Beyond
THE VEIL TO
Heaven

Inexplicable Manifestations
and Signs from a Woman's
Transition to Heaven
while Maintaining Earthly
Life Connections

Ward Edward Barcafer, Jr.

BALBOA
PRESS
A DIVISION OF HAY HOUSE

Balboa Press books may be ordered through booksellers or by contacting:

Balboa Press
A Division of Hay House
1663 Liberty Drive
Bloomington, IN 47403
www.balboapress.com
1 (877) 407-4847

Because of the dynamic nature of the Internet, any web addresses or links contained in this book may have changed since publication and may no longer be valid. The views expressed in this work are solely those of the author and do not necessarily reflect the views of the publisher, and the publisher hereby disclaims any responsibility for them.

The author of this book does not dispense medical advice or prescribe the use of any technique as a form of treatment for physical, emotional, or medical problems without the advice of a physician, either directly or indirectly. The intent of the author is only to offer information of a general nature to help you in your quest for emotional and spiritual well-being. In the event you use any of the information in this book for yourself, which is your constitutional right, the author and the publisher assume no responsibility for your actions.

Any people depicted in stock imagery provided by Thinkstock are models, and such images are being used for illustrative purposes only.
Certain stock imagery © Thinkstock.

Print information available on the last page.

ISBN: 978-1-5043-6892-6 (sc)
ISBN: 978-1-5043-6894-0 (hc)
ISBN: 978-1-5043-6893-3 (e)

Library of Congress Control Number: 2016918741

Balboa Press rev. date: 12/15/2016

CONTENTS

God saw you getting tired and a cure was not to be,
So he put His arms around you and said, "Come to me."
–Author Unknown

PREFACE

Throughout the ages people have wondered whether there is life after death. I certainly have wondered about this myself; probably everyone on earth has wondered, at some time or another, what will become of them after they die. As someone once said, "Is this all there is?" We read about the ones who have died on the operating table or at home but have come back after going somewhere and have said they saw shining lights or heavenly angels. What about those who have actually passed on but have not come back to tell their story? How many have actually come through in some manner with their stories from beyond—where they are now, where they are going, or any other first-person details of their life in heaven?

After knowing and loving my wife for over thirty-three years, I was crushed by her sudden death after a short illness that should have been recoverable. The question I asked myself was why? I have now found the answer, as you will read in the following pages.

Suzette Delashmet Shockley-Barcafer passed from this life on February 2, 2016, at 3:07 p.m. at the age of sixty-nine.

This is her true story, as told to me, Ward Edward Barcafer, Jr., through journaling on numerous occasions.

INTRODUCTION

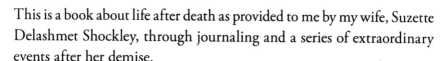

This is a book about life after death as provided to me by my wife, Suzette Delashmet Shockley, through journaling and a series of extraordinary events after her demise.

I believe, and Suz (or Sue, as I and she sometimes called herself) believes, that if only one person can save himself or herself from the completely overwhelming sorrow and utter grief that comes from the death of a loved one, this whole endeavor is worthwhile.

When certain events started to happen, I was in disbelief—I hadn't known or even thought about life after death—so I turned to research and listened for answers to see what was happening. In reading and talking with people who did believe in life after death, I kept an open mind.

There's not a doubt in my mind that some of the events came from another world, as you will see. The events that occurred are not able to happen in the world in which we live. As they happened, one by one, it made sense to me because it was a continuing series of events, I saw something out of the ordinary was happening; in fact, it was very extraordinary and could not be of a human perspective.

I now know that when a person loses a good friend, spouse, child, or other loving relationship, the deceased person can "come through" and communicate. I believe that the stronger the love vibration between the one who has passed and the one left behind, the easier and stronger the connection between them will be.

Suzette had a remarkable life. She was interested in cosmetics to look nice from a young age, and that is why, for all of her adult life, she looked about twenty years younger than her actual age. People she met could not believe her real age. After college, she developed several businesses. One was in Vermont, raising her own sheep for their wool, which she then had dyed and cast into yarn, from which rugs and sweaters were made and sold on a commercial basis. After moving to Colorado, another business was the designing, manufacturing, and hand-painting of jewelry that she sold to stores throughout the West and Midwest. She had a remarkable design and color talent for designing jewelry, gift cards, flowers, and other like items. At one time her interests were varied—real estate sales, mortgage sales, cosmetic sales, and day trading. She was very successful in all of these endeavors due to her love of people.

My name is Ward Edward Barcafer Jr. and I have known and loved Suzette for over thirty-three years; we were married for thirty-one years. In fact, our love merged into unconditional love over that time. After a divorce some years ago, I wanted to find a life partner—not any life partner but a special person I could love and share our life together. I found that in Suz. I had dated many nice women, but I could not find the special one. One Friday night, even though I had gone to several singles dances previously, I decided at the last minute to attend one that was in a remote part of town.

After I was there for a few minutes, two women walked in together. I'd seen one of them at many singles dances but not the other—she'd never attended a singles dance and had been reluctant to go, but her friend talked her into this one. That was Suzette. When she walked in and I saw the way she presented herself, I thought, *Maybe this is the one.* We danced together the whole evening and then decided to see each other again. I found out later that she too was looking for someone with whom she could join together in a common bond.

If I had decided not to go to this dance or if Suzette had declined her friend's invitation, we never would have met. Was this a coincidence, or was it meant to be? I believe that God put us together. I say that because several times in my life, I've felt interventions—when I desired something badly enough and long enough, it seemed to manifest.

For example, years ago I went deer hunting in the Colorado mountains. I was by myself, and after parking on a deserted dirt road,

I walked up a hill not too far from the car and saw a large male deer. I was young; now I don't feel comfortable going hunting any longer. But back then, deer season was a part of living in Colorado for many people, just as it is today. I was able to shoot the deer, but it dropped down into a small gully. It was a big animal, and there was not any way I could bring this deer up from the gully and back to the car by myself. I had gone to church all of my life and felt I had learned to pray. My feeling on prayers was that a person can pray for any just desire within reason. Maybe God will provide and maybe not, depending on His intentions for us. Anyway, I asked God to find a way that I could bring this deer back to my car, as I was not going to leave the deer on the mountain.

As I was praying, a man in a red hooded sweatshirt approached from over a small hill. He said, "I'm not hunting. I'll help you." We got a long tree branch and tied the deer's legs together on the branch. Together, we carried it over our shoulders up from the gully to the road. I thanked him and said, "What do I owe you?" He said, "Nothing. When you find someone else who needs help, just help them." With that, he walked back over the hill. This was a desolate area, and I had not seen another person or car that morning. Was that an angel sent to me while I was praying? Many other things similar to this have happened to me.

Suz knew she had a car angel. One time when she lived in Vermont, she had to drive back home in the dead of the night on a deserted mountain road in a blizzard. Her car slipped off the road into a snow-filled ditch and became stuck. She wondered if she would freeze to death. She prayed, and all of a sudden a large county truck appeared, stopped, and pulled her car out of the ditch. The driver said she was lucky because he usually never went down that county road and was never out that late.

Another time, her Volkswagen threw an engine belt on a lonely road, but very shortly after that, a mechanic drove by, offered to go to a nearby gas station, bought a belt, and installed it for her. Several times when she blew a tire, someone always came by who would change it for her.

So one thing we had in common was that we both felt God's intervention in our lives.

Like many people, I grew up wanting the material things in life—money, houses, and cars; all that I thought were the important things in life. Even though I went to Sunday school and then church on a fairly regular basis, I felt there was something missing in the teachings of "organized" religion.

I have always thought in my heart that God is a loving God. At an older age, I started looking at other churches and found one that prescribed that God was a loving God and that "deeply, all people are one in God's eyes". But even with that, I didn't seem to change that much, other than to respect my fellow humans more. Sue's sudden death and the events that have happened since have changed my beliefs completely.

Through all of these happenings, I came to believe that Sue was telling me that she was fine and alive in another place and that I shouldn't grieve over her because there is truly life after death. I came to realize that even though her physical body was left behind, her consciousness, personality, and spirit live on.

Instead of just believing that there is probably a Higher Intelligence, a Source, that created the earth and the universe, I now know there is a loving Creator that we call God who has created us all. The emotion of love is the highest emotion of all, and my belief now is that God has all-consuming love for his creation and wants to see us all develop that love to the best of our abilities.

Sue told me that I should continue my life on earth and help my fellow humans and we will join in the hereafter. This is also evidenced in the research I found.

After all these experiences, my consciousness has completely shifted. I now have more compassion for other people, more sense of purpose in life, and a willingness to help others as best as I can. I now believe that death on this planet has allowed a new beginning for the spirits of the departed; that their beings, their personalities, and who they are does not change; they only lose their physical presence.

Sue and I want this book written to tell her story in hope that this will help others overcome their grief over the passing of a loved one. For some, maybe this will be just "food for thought," but if it intrigues you to think further about and investigate life after death, it also will be worthwhile.

It is not the intent of this book to change anyone's view on religion. It is only to suggest that you may want to investigate this life-after-death communication by reading more about it. I have provided a suggested reading list at the back of this book.

This is Sue's story, told to me through my mind and by journaling in the early morning. I think I am receiving her messages because over the years we developed a true unconditional love and respect for each other. However, as quantum physics teaches, we may all be vibrational beings in this universe. I believe that if the vibrations from your loved one in heaven and your own vibrations are close enough, communication is possible. I also believe, as the Bible says, that God is love, and the high vibrations of love that Sue and I had and still have for each other enable us to communicate in this manner.

I'd never heard or thought about the possibility of life after death. I was brought up to believe that when we die that death was final. These dramatic happenings that I will describe were so out of this world and strange that I had to research after-death communication (ADC), and I found a number of books and articles on it, even some references to the Middle Ages, that described many of the same events that I was witnessing.

As I have discussed these events with other people, I've found that many have had a similar experience but have been reluctant to share it out of concern that they would be shunned, perhaps even by their families.

There seems to be a pattern to these activities; our loved ones show us that death is not an end but a new beginning, that they indeed are alive in another domain that we and the Bible call heaven.

In my research I found that many such incidences and events, such as I describe in this book, are quite common to ADC, just like reports of near-death experiences (NDE) are quite similar. This continuity led me to believe in the possibility of a renewed life in another dimension or world.

Sue's thoughts and dictation of these notes to me were not vocal;

they came through my mind, usually in the early morning, as a series of distinct sentences. I write them down in my notebooks and then type them up, day to day, in chapter form.

Many of the stimulating books I found to further my knowledge and solidify my thinking have stories similar to Sue's. Again, I have provided a suggested reading list at the back of this book.

Ward Edward Barcafer Jr.

Chapter 1

DEVASTATION

This book is primarily composed of my day-to-day journaling of my talks with Sue, together with some extraordinary happenings. Her voice has a little different vocabulary than mine, and many of her words are not my normal ones. A few of her words are redundant, but I faithfully recorded them as they came to me. In the early mornings and sometimes during the day or when I am in bed at night, her thoughts come through to me. That is why I always have a notebook or tape recorder with me.

Because of my early church upbringing and the passing of friends, family, and others, I knew when my wife passed away—without any real warning and at what I consider the young age of sixty-nine—that she would be gone forever. I had thought she would outlive me, since I am older. I was completely in shock that I would never be with her again and enjoy our old age together.

Devastation and grief hit me like a ton of bricks. I could not believe she was gone. I walked out of the hospital's ICU area and walked sadly down the long and lonely corridor. I left the hospital in a daze, realizing I would never go to the hospital again. When I got home and opened the door, my wife and friend was no longer there to welcome me. The house was dark and lonely, and that first night I just looked at her nightgown and the clothes she had worn before going to the hospital. I could not believe that she would not be coming back. Even now as I write this, I am thinking back to that night.

You will read about her illness, her brain tumor operation, and her extraordinary life. She was at home after her brain tumor operation and seemingly was getting along nicely with various types of therapy, although she was confined to a wheelchair.

About midnight on February 1, she awakened me because she was experiencing shortness of breath, pain in her shoulders, and dizziness. When she had gone to bed earlier, she had started to have pain in her shoulders and wanted liniment rubbed on them to ease the pain. This was the first time that this had happened. As I sat her up on the side of the bed, I knew something was terribly wrong. I tried to take her temperature, but she could not keep the thermometer in her mouth. She seemed extremely dazed and could not talk, so I immediately called 911.

On this night, we were having the strongest blizzard of the year. The 911 operator told me to keep the porch light on so the ambulance and fire truck could find our house in the cul-de-sac in the blizzard. She was sending both vehicles due to the weather conditions. In a few minutes, the firemen arrived, and I was so glad to see them show up. Four of them took charge. They saw that Sue could not walk, so two of them carried her, almost like they would a baby, even though she weighed 126 pounds and was five foot six. They took her to the ambulance through the blizzard. My Jeep was parked outside, so after Sue was safely in the ambulance, they took the time to scoop the snow off my car and start it up. I was so impressed with their actions.

In the emergency room, Sue seemed fine, and I waited while they took many tests. We talked, and she was not in any pain. After these tests, which did not show any problems, the nurses wanted her to remain in the hospital overnight. I walked out into the raging blizzard to get a few hours sleep at home.

The next morning, I went back to the hospital and learned that Sue was in the intensive care unit. I was dumbfounded, as I expected her to be in a regular hospital room. In the ICU, I was told they had found blood clots in and near her heart. The doctor stated that with the proper blood thinning, she should be fine to go home in a couple of days. Sue was awake, talking, and seemed her old self again. Of course, she had IVs, oxygen, and a catheter and was hooked up to all of the monitors they use in the ICU.

I was still quite tired after only a few hours sleep, so I went back home for more rest. Later, as I was about to go back to the hospital, I received a phone call from the hospital chaplain. He said that Sue's heart had stopped, but they were doing resuscitation, and I should come over right away. When I got there about twenty-five minutes later, the chaplain said that her heart had started again but then stopped just before I arrived. He said that she just suddenly rolled over, and her heart stopped again.

Looking back on it, I feel that all of the pain of the physical resuscitation, along with the pain and stress of her brain tumor operation, was just too much for her. She did not want any more of it. Her doctor had mentioned that perhaps in six months, he might or might not have to go in and drain some fluid. I don't think she could have withstood that. In the ICU I'm sure she thought everything was starting all over again. She was always concerned about whether she would ever get her old life back. At that time, I am sure she did not know or care if there was anything beyond this earthly life.

The doctors and nurses—by now several were in the room—were trying frantically to resuscitate her.

The chaplain asked if I wanted to go in, but I could see by all of the activity that I would be in the way. Anyway, I could not handle seeing the resuscitation attempts. Every few minutes, the nurses would change as they became tired. I watched through the doorway, and it broke my heart to see all of them working at resuscitating her and the heart monitor flatlining, starting up again, and flatlining. I understand that they had to do physical resuscitation, as a heart does not have any specific electrolytes inside the cell, and a machine would have just burned the heart.

Finally, the doctor came out and told me they had lost her, and there was no reason to continue the process. The head nurse who had been taking care of Sue all morning started crying uncontrollably. I was in complete shock and disbelief; I'd thought she would recover, be well, and her heart would be normal in a few days. My lovely wife was gone in the space of twenty-four hours. Her body was lying there in the hospital bed, lifeless. I was not even able to say good-bye or hold her hand before she passed, as there was so much going on with all the processes taking place that there was no room for me to be close to her.

The nurses wanted me to wait outside while they cleaned her up. After they were through, I went in to see her. I said to the nurse, "Could you please take the metal brace from Sue's mouth?" It was still in place, as air had been forced through it in hope of giving Sue enough oxygen.

"It needs to stay in place," she said, "until the coroner gets here."

I flinched at the word *coroner*, as it meant Sue was truly gone.

I stood with her for a little while, really not still believing she was gone from my life forever. I wanted to do something, but there was nothing I could do. I kissed her forehead in good-bye. As I mentioned, I walked out of the hospital in full grief, knowing that I was leaving her there, and she was not coming home with me ever again. Little did I realize the events that soon would take place.

I had never heard of after-death communication (ADC). At that moment, I knew I would never see or hear from Sue again. Boy, was I wrong.

Chapter 2

BEGINNINGS

In the late fall of 2014, Sue started to become dizzy and lose her balance occasionally during the day but not every day. She and I felt that it was probably temporary, but we decided to see a doctor who knew her history. The doctor suggested that it might be the beginning of multiple sclerosis (MS) or some other degenerative disease, but he wanted to take a wait-and-see attitude to see if any other symptoms developed.

Sue was home alone, as we had no relatives living close by. I had to work and could only come home during the day every once in a while. I came home one afternoon, and just as I entered the door, I heard her cry out for help. I rushed into the kitchen and found her on the kitchen floor, so weak she could not get up. She had been cooking dinner and just keeled over. Her face, normally very nice and soft-looking, was contorted in shock and pain, and her hair and clothes were covered with soil from the large potted flowers that we kept on the kitchen floor—her head had glanced off the side of the flower pot, spilling the dirt. I could not believe my eyes. I gingerly lifted her up. Thank goodness she was not injured. She felt better later and wanted to wait until the next day to see the doctor.

Again, the doctors did tests but could not find anything wrong. Later that year, she fell out of bed during the night, landed hard, and broke her forearm; she was in a cast for several weeks. The doctors suggested that maybe she should get an MRI of her head at some point. During the Christmas holidays, she seemed fine.

In January 2015, I was home during the day and heard her scream.

She had fallen down the short flight of basement stairs, hit her head, and landed partially on top of a three-foot tree made of pinecones that had not yet been put away in storage. She was lying among some of the broken-off pine cones that were like stickers; fortunately, she was not hurt by the cones. As we were both concerned by her fall, I drove her to a hospital emergency room for a checkup.

A CT scan found a large mass in her brain. That night, an MRI showed a large tumor with an adjacent cyst. Back in early 2014, if she'd had an MRI, the radiation possibly could have killed the tumor while it was smaller. The tumor was a *schwannoma*, which is a benign nerve sheath tumor composed of Schwann cells, which normally produce insulating a myelin sheath that covers peripheral nerves. (More on this later.) As it turned out, even though it was benign, the size necessitated brain surgery.

The first event that showed me that Sue had moved on to another place that we call heaven was strange to me until I realized that what happened was from Sue herself. In fact, when these events started to happen, I was in disbelief and tried to find answers from other sources, researching to see what was happening. I kept an open mind as I spoke with people who believed in life after death. One such person was a minister of a church; he understood from other sources that what was happening to me was fully conceivable. Some of these events definitely came from another world. Common sense says they are not able to happen in this world, but they did.

As these activities continued to happen, one by one, it made sense to me because I saw that something was happening that was extraordinary. I know now that when a person loses a good friend, a spouse, a child, or anyone else they hold dear that the deceased person can come through, provided there was a loving relationship that permits love vibrations to come forth from both the deceased and the still living. As mentioned, Sue and I had an unconditional loving relationship. I do not know if someone can come through without a loving relationship, as that was not our situation. (Maybe someone can figure that out.) I have found out that the higher the love vibration between the one who has passed and the one left behind, the easier and stronger the connection between them will be.

Suzette had a remarkable life but one that was too short—sixty-nine years; it seems many years too short to me. I now understand, however, that God—Higher Intelligence, Creator, whatever name you give to the Supreme Being who created the universe—has a destiny for each of us, and there is a reason for everything.

The first event of many occurred on Tuesday night, February 2, 2016.

As I mentioned, Sue passed away on Tuesday, February 2, at 3:07 in the afternoon.

Later that Tuesday, at sometime during the night after I had been asleep for a little while, I awakened and could not get back to sleep. I was fully awake. I was startled when in my mind's eye, I saw Sue's face; it was very shadowy, but it had changed a little. Her left eye was affected by her brain operation. She could not blink, and a gold weight had been inserted into her upper eyelid to enable her to close her eyelid at will. On this night, her left eye was closed but it did not look the way it looked prior to her passing. I heard her speak—coming from my mind, not in a voice. She wanted me to go to sleep and said she loved me for the way I had taken care of her after her operation. She said that I should now take care of myself, and she would be with me. I should not concern myself about her passing because she was with me now, and I should sleep soundly from now on.

She said one of the reasons she came to me was because she could feel that I was very distraught. She said that she would now be with me because of our unconditional love for each other, as well as being with anyone else if she desired. She could do other things and still be with me. She also said that her body had been tired, and she'd been ready to go because at the hospital it appeared that all of her pain and emotional shock was starting all over again.

She was concerned that I if did not get over her passing it would affect my health, particularly after all of the stress of taking care of her in the last few months. She also wanted me to know that she was happy, even joyful, where she was, and I should not be concerned anymore about her passing, as she could be with me from time to time. I should sleep and relax.

A kind of relaxed and peaceful feeling came over me, and I slept soundly that night for several hours.

This was the beginning of many extraordinary and inexplicable events over the next several months. (You will read about these events in my journaling of her thoughts, feelings, and whereabouts after her passing.) Sue and I had a wonderful life together. I firmly believe that our unconditional love vibrations for each other have made this connection possible. In my mind, there is truly life after death. What follows are notes that I took on the events.

Thursday Morning, February 4, Journaling

[I am sitting in my home office this morning as I write this. This office is located in a downstairs room that was originally a bedroom. It is quiet and away from the street and any neighborhood noise. On the wall behind my computer monitor is a window that looks out on the backyard, and when the shade is up I can sometimes see squirrels and birds in the yard. It is a very pleasant place to work, and I normally work in the evening.

I live alone now but heard her voice again last night coming through my mind. I just knew it was her because it was a completely different feeling from my own thoughts. It had the same inflection of her voice that I knew so well. She has a larger vocabulary than I have developed and uses words that I do not commonly use in my speech or thinking. She wants me to write down her thoughts in a notebook.]

[Please remember that this is coming through my mind and not an actual voice. Also, some of the beginnings and endings of each of these messages might seem redundant, but I want to tell it word for word.]

[Sue, are you there?]

Yes, I am here with you. I will always be with you, even though I am everywhere else too. Please take it easy. I love you more and more now. Thank you for taking care of me beyond what anyone else would do. It is a little hard for me to come through since this is so new. Please be patient with me, and I will have stronger ways of talking with you eventually. I will be with you the rest of your life, helping you as you have helped me. I think it was cute of you to want a lock of my hair and buying the fingerprint piece that they will take prior to my cremation.

Please do not worry about me. I am at peace. Again, please take care of yourself, and do not stress any more over my passing. You did all the best that you could do for me while I was alive. I just got tired. I will give you a sign one day, maybe sooner than later, that you will understand. Please take care of yourself. I am well. Good-bye for now.

Thursday Night, February 4, Flashing Lights

[Sue said that she would give me a sign, maybe sooner than later.

I was sitting in our dining room at the table in the evening and had just turned on the vaulted-ceiling floodlights—a set of two floods on the east side of the ceiling and a set of three on the west side of the ceiling. All of the sudden, they started flashing at a much brighter intensity than the normal light output and brighter than they have during the sixteen years we have lived here. The lights flashed erratically from one bulb to another, like an ambulance's or police car's flashing lights. They were very bright, very fast, jumping from one bulb to another a fraction of a second apart. First the right bulb would flash, then the third, back to the second and so on—like *bang, bang, bang.*

They were much brighter than normal and had never flashed before. That kept on until I turned them off. I was dumbfounded, but because Sue had said that morning that she would give me a sign to show me she was "alive and well," I knew that was her, but I did not know what to make of it. I took this to mean that she could control electricity. At that time, I really did not know what was going on. I was startled, and in the back of my mind, I still wondered if that was Sue.]

Friday Morning, February 5

[Sue, I loved you and still love you so much.]
Please take care of yourself now. I know you are upset. I can feel

it. Please take care of yourself and enjoy the rest of your life. You did take care of me to the best of your ability, which was much greater than I ever expected or should have expected. You did everything right and much more so. We had a great time together, saw and did many things. I know you really loved me, and I was trying my best to love you, but as you know, I had a hard time loving myself because of my childhood background. But at last, I learned to love you very much and was surprised that I could do that. I finally learned how to love myself and love you.

Perhaps that was what my soul needed—why I was put on earth and why I met you because you helped me learn to love. Please start your day, relax, take care of yourself, and we will talk again.

[What about the lights?]

Yes, that was me. I have been trying to tell you that I am fine now. I was tired and hurting but not now. Thank you for helping me and all of the things you did, taking me relentlessly to all of the doctor's appointments and watching over me.

Friday Night, February 5, Flashing Lights Again

[In the late evening, again as I sat at the dining room table, I turned the vaulted-ceiling lights on, and again the flashing lights repeated themselves in the exact manner as the night before until I turned them off. They went on and off, on and off, from extremely bright to dim. I am catching up on my journal notes after many days, and the lights have never flashed again. The bulbs have been working normally as they have for sixteen years. I really did not know what was happening, so I had to find out what was going on. I tried to find out through some books and an Internet site on life after death. It seems that many other people over the years have had similar experiences. I was soon to see even more dramatic signs from Sue as we move on in the days ahead.

That started me on my journey of exploring the world of the afterlife in many ways—through books, the Internet, and my church. Again, I had to know what was going on. I read a book that said that one of the ways the departed show their loved ones that they are all right and in another life is by means of electrical phenomena, like flashing lights. It is easy for them to handle electric current as well as other means, such as a radio, TV, or a computer that is operated by electricity.

Just as some human energy can affect electrical systems, so can the energy of spirits through an electrical magnetic force. Some humans, in fact, can't wear watches and can even affect electrical appliances. Working with nonphysical energy is the easiest way for spirits to affect our physical reality.

I have also read that electromagnetic fields are regarded as real and an independent part of our physical world and that a robust realist view of consciousness is that it is more on a par with electromagnetic fields than with life. This might mean that at death, the brain ceases to function, but consciousness, identity, and personality move on. This would make sense to me with all of the near-death experiences (NDEs) we read about, people moving to heaven and coming back, when their brains have shown no activity. This would also allow for complete passing, called after-death experience (ADE), as consciousness would flow out from the body and brain.]

Sunday Morning, February 7

[Hi, I love you.]

And I love you. Thank you for taking care of me when I needed it. Now please take care of yourself. Gain some weight, relax, and in a little while you will be able to slow down. Again, relax and enjoy the rest of your life. I am going to be with you as long as you want me to. Now is the time to take care of you.

Until you get the recorder you ordered, please keep this book with you so that you can jot down my thoughts as they come to you. Again, this is our mutual love together in a high density that enables me to come through to you. Love is a vibration that enables this conversation. I am happy, joyful, [and] well in your terms, so please relax and get better. You have a long life ahead; I can see that. You have free will. I cannot and would not interfere with that. I love you and did not know how much your shoulders hurt from getting me off the bed and [into] the bathroom. As you thought, had I known I probably would not have gone to the bathroom as much, so there also might have been complications then.

Please, now go to church if you want, and we will talk again.

Love,

Suz

Don't be sad. I am right here with you, although you can't see me. We will talk all we want. That is why I know what you are doing. Maybe I can show myself eventually, but not yet; maybe sooner than later. There are many dimensions, just like grade school and high school in your world. We go up from one to the other. Just pretend I am with you, because I am. Don't cry. One of these days you will see me in person. I don't know when, but I promise.

Chapter 3

FIRST VISUAL CONTACT

Tuesday Morning, February 9

[Hi, are you there]

Good morning. I know you slept pretty well, and I am thankful for that. Maybe now you can start relaxing, knowing that I am with you, and start enjoying life. As I mentioned last night, scientists cannot comprehend what the universe is all about. It is so huge, immense, and much more than they know, far reaching into what you call space, as you know it.

I am glad that you found that picture of *The Narrow Gate* and will hang it up in the house to give you solace that I am alive in my world now and that I am me and live in peace and joy. I know that you have many questions and are afraid of asking them, but you will be more comfortable in a while and ask me what I can answer.

As I mentioned, there are many layers where I am, and it is just like the layers of grade school, high school, and so forth. But all are joy and happiness and love. I will show you myself when the time comes in some way, but it is too soon for both of us. Be patient, please relax, and let your world flow like, as you know, downstream and not paddling upstream. I know you have a lot you want to do, so please, we will go now. Good-bye.

[*Note:* The Narrow Gate *painting shows women leaving their worldly possessions behind and floating upward toward heaven. The Narrow Gate,* ©2016 Sonya Shannon.]

Tuesday Evening, February 9

[Sue, it's been a tough day. I don't know why my phone would not work. The e-mail would not work.]

I understand that you are frustrated over my not being there with you as I have been for thirty-three years. It is nice that you are going to make an album of my photos as a reminder of our physical life together. It is also nice that you are going to let Tracy have some of my jewelry, and it is nice that you are going to give some of my therapy items away to people that need them and maybe cannot afford them. That angel picture will remind you that I did let go of my possessions and my earthly concerns when I rose up.

I now have to talk with you with your earthly vocabulary, so I realize that some of my thoughts may not come through as clearly as I would like them to, but we will proceed, and you will know that we are so close that you will understand what I am saying. Please relax, and don't be as upset as you have been this week. I am here. I love you and will always be here as long as you want me to.

Good night, dear.

Wednesday Morning, February 10

[Good morning.]

Good morning. I wish you were not so upset. I am in a better place. I will be with you more than anyone else since our love vibrations toward each other are almost identical. I have more affinity for your vibrations than anyone else since you loved me—really loved me—and took good care of me. We were really inseparable, although I don't think we looked at it that way at the time. Please do not think of my core body lying in the hospital, as it makes you sad, and you know that I am all right. My earthly body, my shell, if you want to call it that, was not doing me any good any longer. I came to earth to do what I had to do. I needed to learn how to love and after many, many years achieved that through you.

Please just relax, live your life, and think of me and our years together, if you want to. You took extremely good care of me over the years and especially these last few months. Most people would have not done what you did for me and needed to do. I love you, and you deserve it. As the movie went, "Love is a many splendored thing." Again, I am repeating myself, but please take care of yourself. We will get deeper into my situation—that is, where I am—when the time comes. I still want to show myself to you, but I don't know yet in which manner or time is best for you. Please get along with your life and work today, and we will talk again soon. Remember, I am always with you and have no judgment on what you do.

Thanks.

Sue

Thursday Morning, February 11

Good morning.

[Where are you?]

It is impossible to describe now, in 2016, because the human consciousness has not developed to the degree of understanding necessary to understand. Just realize that I am me, the person you knew on earth and loved and cherished and the person that loved and loves you very much. You took good care of me and kept my spirits up when I needed your love and helped the most in the last few days and especially after my operation. Do you have any other questions now?

[You have told me that you are happy and filled with joy.]

It is unbelievable how much happiness I now feel. I think a while back you had a feeling of joy for a few seconds. Well, I have that beautiful feeling of lightness and joy all of the time. It is a beautiful feeling, all complete and satisfying. Please don't cry for me anymore. You know that I am well and happy and looking over you. We had beautiful times together, and looking back, I did not realize sometimes the fun and togetherness we shared. You don't have to talk with me all of the time if you don't want to. Just be quiet, silent, and meditate for me and with me. Silence sometimes is golden, as they say.

But please, by all means communicate with me when you want

to and as much as you want. I am always here for you because of our mutual love and affection. On a personal note, thank you for sending some of my jewelry and the opal ring to my mother. I am glad you got a good night's sleep last night after the week and hope you will take care of yourself from now on, as you know I am happy and content.

[Where do you go from here?]

Where my spirit and personality finally end up I do not know now, but I do know it will be beautiful, wherever I end up. Maybe just here. As time progresses, your time, I will let you know. But don't worry, as my time on earth is over and the bad things—hurt, worry, disease of the body and mind—are all over for me. I loved my life on earth, and who knows where I will go from here. I think my soul has something to do with that. I learned many lessons while I was alive, and whether I need more learning, I just do not know at this time. Please get on with your day, and we will talk again.

Thursday Night, February 11

Take care of yourself. I am going to help you through this emotional time. Just think now that I am talking like I am in another room, and we are talking on the telephone. You can't see me, but we can communicate. Our vibrations are the same, and that is why we can communicate with each other. So take it easy and relax, and go to bed early. We will talk again soon.

Friday Morning, February 12, First Visual Sighting

[I wear a sleeping mask many times at night so I don't wake up in the early morning, as we have skylights in our bedroom.

Last night I awoke at 4:00 a.m., and a voice in my mind said that there was a shadowy figure standing at the foot of my bed. I heard in my mind a voice say, "Take off your mask so you can see me." I did, and at the foot of my bed on the right side, just for a fraction of a second, there was a dark fuzzy form of a person about Sue's height. It was black in the bedroom, so I could not see if there was any color. In a split-second the fuzzy form was gone. A voice in my mind said, "I could not stay longer." As a human being, I have goose bumps as I think of this, although in my heart I know it was Sue. Where she comes from or how, we might not yet know.]

[Was that you last night?]

Yes, that was me.

[I want to ask how you can come.]

I really don't know myself. I just thought that I would give you a sign of being myself in person, as I told you and promised I would. I just had the thought to come and see you, and it happened. I love you and wanted to show you that I am alive in my world so you would not continue to worry and stress out when you think of our memories and our life together and my transition. You look at my things, my clothes, and get emotionally upset when you should not. I am well, know what is going on in your world with you, and wish you to continue your life in as happy a manner as you can now. I am always with you, have no judgment, and wish you a happy life for what is left of your life on earth.

Please don't continue to get emotionally upset as it is not necessary, as you know. I will come again, time to time. Don't wear your sleeping mask before 5:00 a.m., and I can have you see me for a fraction longer. Look for other signs, even during the day. The reason that I do this [signs] is so you realize that I am alive and in a different place, that my personality is me. Please don't think of my body lying in the hospital morgue, as it makes you sad, and you know that I am all right.

See you soon and talk to you.

Sue

Monday Morning, February 15

[Hello, What do you want to talk about]

I did what I came here [earth] to achieve. That was to feel love, which I did through you, and now I was ready to go. Thank you very much for what you gave me. May be back again; I do not know now. But as long as we have the vibrations of love between us, even when you pass on, we will be together.

When the tape recorder comes, keep it with you so you can jot down my thoughts during the day as you go about your business. As I have mentioned, I will be here as long as you want me to. Talk with you later. Have a good day, and please do not get upset when you pick up my ashes. Remember it is just my shell now. It is not me.

What do you want to ask me? Ask me anything. I just like talking to you.

[I miss you.]

And I miss you too. I wish you would not be so sad. I know that I am not there in person, but I am still with you, and we can talk through your mind.

[I guess I can't ask you yet where you are because, as you say, it really is beyond my comprehension. I wonder if you will come back to earth and be born again in spirit and soul as another person.]

I don't know at this time. My transition is too new. I am only now starting to realize where I am, but I am happy, joyful, like being on a cloud, but I am not on a cloud.

This is a wonderful experience, however I wish we could be have been together a little while longer while I was on earth as your wife and friend, but it was not to be. My last few months were hell on earth, although my mind was solid, firm, and worked just as before, but my body deserted me. And of course, that will happen to all on earth at some point in time. I am only being realistic in my thinking, but while you are whole and happy, why not live a full life and enjoy your beautiful experience, as earth is a beautiful place. Please go about your business and we will talk later. Do what you want with my things. I know you will be careful and do the right thing.

Tuesday Morning, February 16

[Good morning.]

Good morning. How are you? In my case, I am fine and love you. I am in another plane and can know what you are thinking and doing. I also have no judgments, as love does not allow for judgments. For the first time in my existence, I have very unconditional love. I enjoy our talks and hope you will continue each morning. Have a good day today. I know you have a lot you want to do today. Please don't ask me where I am because you would not understand, could not understand, because of the limited consciousness of the planet earth.

I am glad you are reading and learning about life after death. In these books it mentions that sometimes the nonphysical person can communicate with the physical person due to the same vibrations, and I add the vibrations are of love because the universe is love.

Call the universe God if you will; the name does not matter. It is all *one*. I am closer than you think. You just cannot see me; however, I am with you and can still do everything that my spirit and soul want me to do. I am also glad that you are listening to some DVDs about life after death, as it is not only comforting to you but is helping to enlighten you as to the nonphysical.

[What will you do now?]

I don't yet really know. My spirit and my soul are in transition to something else. It does not matter what happens further to and for me, as everything is joy and light, and I instinctively know it will always be so. Time now does not matter as it does on earth. Time is not important to the universe. I am too new at this and wait upon my future, but what is important is that we can communicate with each other.

I love you, and you love me, so where I am is not that important to our continuing relationship. You have a lot you want to do today so please start, as you know we can talk throughout your day. I know that sometimes it is hard for you to realize that I am always there for you, but as time goes on you will realize that I am close. Think of me often, and you will get to know that I am as close to you now as when I was alive on earth.

We will still do things together, just as if I were in another room in the house, and you could not see me from the room you are in. Think about that, and you will feel closer to me. Thank you for all of the things you did for me after my operation. I did not realize at the time all of the things you did and were doing, but I see it now. Thank you, thank you, thank you. So long for now.

Friday Morning, February 19

[Hi. Are you there?]

Yes, I am here and will be here for you always. I am sorry you are not feeling good now. It will pass. I am glad that you are getting the insurance money because it will help you with your finances and enable you to relax a bit.

[I miss you terribly.]

I know that, and you can't help it after our knowing each other and living together for thirty-three years. But take care of yourself, as you have many good years of life left before you join me.

[Will I ever see you again?]

That means what you mean about seeing me. I have tried to come to you in the night but it is still hard; however, it will work out at some point. With our love, after you do pass on, we can be together again in spirit. I had a hard time loving growing up, but I learned to love you deeply.

[Why did you leave me?]

It turned out to be the best thing, as my body was getting worn out after the operation. As you know, I could not be myself physically and was dependent on others, who did take care of me, but I have always been independent in my physical living, and I just could not stand the dependence that I was living. I couldn't be myself physically, and it really bugged me. Even though it was a little hard in the last few hours, it has been for the best.

[Note: We both think God intervened, as not only was it Sue's time, but I was fifteen years older. She feels that without any living relatives in her older age, she would have been left with strangers who did not know her, and she was afraid that she could be left for years in the back room of a nursing home with a feeding tube in her stomach. This is what a dietician had said to her before the operation when she was having a rough time digesting her food from an unrelated illness.

Why someone in the medical profession would scare her like that is unbelievable. In another chapter, I will discuss her brain tumor operation and the problems in detail to help anyone in that situation understand the procedures.

One of the outcomes of the operation was her inability to swallow food, although it was getting a little better in her final days. She had a feeding tube in her stomach, although we managed that properly. So you can see the concern weighing on her mind after the unfortunate statement from the dietician. We both knew God understood the situation, and that is one of the reasons He released her from this earthly life, as well as that her soul work on this earth was completed.]

You are free to do what you want now, and that makes me happy, and I am free as a bird and joyful. Thank you for the months and months of taking care of me, almost on an hourly basis. I did not realize at the time everything you did, as much of it was outside of the house— going shopping, looking after my physical needs, and other things. I did not know that your shoulders were hurting after a while due to lifting me up all of the time. I enjoyed you the last six months after the operation, even though I was a bit of a pain in the neck. It was, though, as you thought, frustration that I could not handle myself physically. Talk to you later. You have things to do today. Good-bye. Love you.

Chapter 4

MATERIALIZATIONS/
ADDITIONAL CONTACTS

Saturday Morning. February 20, Flashing Again

[Hi. I miss you being here when I come home. I love you very much. and you left too soon.]

Hi, It is all right. Did you get my latest sign?

[Last night, I went into the bathroom in the middle of the night, the floodlight above the shower started flashing, but the other two smaller bulbs in the bathroom ceiling did not flash.]

[Yes, I did, but you know that I did believe the first series in the dining room as a sign, the day after you passed out of this physical life.]

Well, I wanted you again to know that I am here with you on the nonphysical level. I am trying to materialize in the middle of the night for a very brief second or so, but I am still trying to see how I can do that. Please go about your work now, as you again have a busy day. When you can, maybe Sunday, just stop and be quiet and meditate, and we will see what happens.

Monday Morning, February 22, Materialization

[On Sunday night, I awakened at 10:50, as I had gone to bed early at 8:00. Sue was, for an instant, kneeling at my bedside and reaching an arm and hand toward me. I had the feeling she was saying hello and giving me an "It's all right now" sign. It took me a fraction of a second to notice that she was about one-half her normal size but wearing a blouse and pants. I said, "Sue, is that you?" And I knew that it was.]

[Was that you?]

Yes, I finally figured out how to materialize just for a fraction of a second. As the time goes on, you will see me for a little longer time and more clearly. I am not going to bother you much at all, but I want you to know that I am all right. Thank you for everything you did for me while I was with you. I love you, and we will talk again. Please go about your work. Good-bye for now.

Tuesday Morning, February 23

[Last night, in the middle of the night, I woke, as I many times do, and I was startled to notice a light coming out of our bathroom. I wondered where this light could be coming from, as I had turned out all of the lights when I went to bed. I got up, and as I got closer, I heard a little beeping sound. We have an alarm box mounted on the wall, but the alarm is disconnected. However, the little electrical signal light is always on inside of a closed lid. The lid had dropped down, which it has never done before as long as we have lived here. By dropping down on the hinges, the light was fully exposed and made a bright light that reflected off the bathroom walls. The beeping sound was coming from the box.]

[Sue, that was you again?]

Yes. I can best show you that I am fine through electrical lights. I did that as another showing to you that I am not dead, as you humans in the earth environment think of death. I am more alive now and looking forward to where the future takes me. I love you, and our life together was beautiful, happy, and fun. You were a great husband to me, and I enjoyed being with you. I loved you then, and I love you now.

You think that you did something wrong and could not hold on to my life at the end, but you did nothing wrong, so don't blame yourself for my passing. It was just my time, although I did not know it at the time. I was scared, but it turned out all right in the end. Please don't stress out anymore, as you know that I am all right. I have tried to show you with many signs that my spirit, my soul, and myself as you know me are still alive but in another dimension.

I can go anywhere I want in the universe, but why would I? I want to be connected to you, as I was when I was alive in your world. I can't stress enough that I am here where I am, and you should not worry and concern yourself about my passing. Please get along on your work, and we can talk tomorrow on your birthday.

Love,

Sue

Wednesday Morning, February 24, Blinking Printer Lights

[Sue has a laptop computer on a stand in the dining room just outside of our kitchen door. I have not moved it yet. Last night I got up in the middle of the night to go into the kitchen to get a glass of water. As I rounded the corner I saw that the light on the printer, which she had not been working, was blinking on and off. Also, the little indicator light on the laptop computer speaker, which was plugged in to a different outlet but turned off, was also blinking on and off.]

[Sue, I was again astonished by this electrical activity. It is hard for me to believe you are still around.]

Please believe it. Yes, these were other signs, and I want to give you more if you want me to. I will continue to give you signs. Please do not be afraid because it is me, your loving wife.

[I do not understand this reincarnation business.]

I don't either. I am now kind of in a blissful, happy, joyful limbo, waiting to see what comes next. I am fine. Please do not worry about me. I am better by far than I was in the last few months after my operation.

[Other than the printer lights, you did not come to me last night. I guess I am expecting too much and hoping too much.]

I did come to you last night, but you were asleep, and I did not want to wake you up. I am glad you had the films put on DVD. I had forgotten them. Remember I love you, and love is forever. I am glad that you got a lot more rest last night. It was good to take the Chrysler back. Now you do not have to worry about it. One less worry for you.

The last few years were tough on me because of my failing health, a lot more than I let on to you because I did not want to worry you. I had some trials in my life before I met you that probably affected my health, but in the end I did become my own person. But as you know from the home movies, we did have a lot of fun together, and I did enjoy my life and my life with you.

I know you don't think so now, in your hurting, but you are a wonderful person and made my life comfortable, fun, and enjoyable in our thirty-three years together. As Abraham says, "I love you very much." Talk to you again soon.

Love,
Suz

[Note: Abraham—a group of obviously evolved nonphysical teachers— speak their broader perspective through Esther Hicks. Abraham-Hicks Publications.]

Thursday Morning, February 25

[Hi, What is going on.]

I did not mention yesterday that I wanted to wish you a happy birthday. I am all right. You do not need to worry anymore about me. I am with you now, although you can't see me. I can see you. Please live your life without worry. Again, I am all right and full of love and joy. Like the print you bought, I have left all of my earthly baggage behind. I am glad you had the tapes of our vacations put on DVDs. I had forgotten some of the things we did. I am glad you are listening to the Abraham-Hicks programs, as they will help you to know that I am okay.

I am glad you are starting to relive the way things are with me and are not as sad anymore. Thank goodness you are now starting to get more sleep. I know that it was a shock to you—and really to me also— the way my passing happened so fast, right out of the blue, so to speak.

Take your time on cleaning up the house, as you have plenty of time to do it. I am right beside you although you can't see me. But I see that you can feel my presence. Thank you for all of the things you did for me to be able to be comfortable when I came home from rehabilitation.

I enjoyed all of the cooking and baking we did in the last six months, although I realize it took you a little time to get used to it. I love you very much. We had good, great times together. You were the love of my life, although I sometimes had a difficult time showing it due to my earlier life while at a college in Vermont. Give my clothes away to whomever you want. I know they will enjoy them as I did also. Talk to you again.

Love,

Suz

Please don't cry, as you know that I am here and okay. That is why I have given you all of the signs that you could not mistake, especially the flashing overhead ceiling lights.

Friday Morning, February 26

[Hi.]

Hi. I am glad you are feeling better and sleeping better. Again, I am fine, and I also am glad you are listening to the Abraham DVDs. They will help you a lot in my passing.

[I miss you so much.]

I know you do. I can feel it, but just remember, as they say, I am in a better place. That saying is a little trite, but nevertheless it is true. I am glad that you are getting, to a degree, over my transition. You know that I am all right, and I want you to know that I miss our physical interaction that we had for thirty-three years. You were and are the light of my life. Thank you for loving me so much. Our love vibrations continue, and that is the main reason that we can communicate now, even when your vibrations are sometimes sad.

I know that you miss me terribly, and I miss you, although it is a happy, joyful experience for me to be able to talk to you like this. I am okay, and now I think you know it. I also know from your human experience that you feel that this a little weird, but it is actually what is happening between us, this loving communication.

Talk to you again soon, as I know you have a lot you want to do today. Again, happy birthday, and I know you will have many more in your lifetime on earth if you take care of yourself. Use the money DVD and that will give you the tools of the law of attraction to keep you going.

Good-bye until next time.

Suz

Saturday Morning, February 27, Another Materialization

[I awakened last night at 10:23 and saw her over the head of my bed with outstretched arms. She was showing her shadowy upper part of her body, and her face was not fully defined in features, but I felt and knew it was Sue. She is showing me she is alive and well in her nonphysical form and place. What a relief to know she is all right.]

[Do you still love me?]

You ask, do I still love you? I love you deeply, deeply, deeply, more than you can imagine, more than I showed when I was with you on planet earth. Because of my background, I had a hard time showing love, although it was always there. We had good, great times together, and as I summarized long ago in that letter to myself about your qualities, I really meant that. We were a perfect fit.

You are feeling a lack of self-worth now because you have been exhausted physically and mentally. Once you begin living for yourself again, your feelings of self-worth will return. Look what you did in life so far—built two businesses practically from scratch (although I did not know you at the time) into the largest of their type in the Rocky Mountain region.

Please do not have difficult emotions about my passing. I am fine, as you know because I came to see you last night at 10:23 as you awakened from a deep sleep. You saw me over the head of your bed with my arms outstretched as to love you. I came just like that the night before, but you awakened too late to see me. I can only now—I say, now—stay for a part of a split second.

I will be here as long as you want me to during your life on earth. According to what you are reading and feeling, we will know each other and be together in the afterlife, as long as our vibrations are strong for each other. Please go about your business today. Love you. Good-bye for now. I wish you would not be so upset when you think of my passing and our life together.

I want you to remember me and our times together, but if you truly believe I am where I am and am happy and joyful, you will not be sad. I want you to enjoy your life and think of our times together as joyful times, and remember: *I am still here.*

[Note: She talks to me through my mind during the day from time to time as I think about it, although when I am engaged with my life, my business, or other things, she does not come through, since my mind is elsewhere.]

Monday Morning, February 29

[Hi.]

Hi.

[I miss you so much. Sometimes at night I get sad that you are not physically here.]

I am glad you are going to see the woman at church and talk over some of the questions you have with her.

I know you have some questions about what I look like now without my physical body. I look like what you want me to look like, whatever age you think of me is what I look like. I am a free spirit, and when I come to you, probably for an instant at night, I will look however you want me to look. I can take any form I want to.

[Are you lonely? Probably a silly question.]

No, I am with God [the Universal Spirit] and dropped my emotional baggage when I moved on. I am seeing things more clearly, and I am living in happiness and joy. I am free of all of the emotional problems that I developed in my earlier life before I met you. I truly am happy, and I do love you very much.

[It is interesting talking to you and not seeing you.]

Yes, I know. But believe that I am here, and if it helps you, think of our talking by telephone. Actually, it is long distance (pun). Please take care of yourself, as you have many good years left before you go from this earth. As I have said, I am limited in talking with you using your earthly vocabulary. I am glad you are starting to relax now and take care of yourself. I miss being with you physically too. Looking back, earth is a beautiful place for earthlings to enjoy. Talk to you again later, as you have many things today you want and need to do. Goodbye, love.

[You are a beautiful, loving person, and I miss you very much.]

Yes, I know. Thanks.

Monday Evening, February 29

[Are you sure you were happy with me in our marriage?]

Yes, of course. I love you very much, and I miss you. You did a lot for me. We had wonderful times together. You remembered every anniversary and birthday with beautiful flowers and cards. You were strong and kept me out of trouble. A precious man and friend. I do not think that I could have found a better husband. I could not believe how good, trusting, friendly, and loving you were to me before and after my operation. I have loved you very much and still do. We had a few little differences like any couple will have over that many years together.

Please put your doubts aside; just realize I enjoyed our life together and all of the material things we had. Please get your emotions together and use the laws of attraction for money. I love you, and I too can pray where I am, and I pray for your safety and well-being. Don't concern yourself with some of my writings when I was down on myself or anything, when I had a tendency to be negative toward life.

Remember we had a wonderful life together, more than I could have imagined with anyone else. If we didn't have, we probably would not be talking now, because the love vibrations we have for one another are our communication channel. Please relax, and have a nice sleep tonight. See ya.

Love,

Suz

I am glad you are finding the pictures of me, and you are going to make a scrapbook of my life on earth.

Tuesday Morning, March 1

[You didn't come to see me last night.]

Yes, I did, but you were asleep, and I did not want to wake you.

[I hope you don't think that I caused you more grief than happiness in our years together.]

Of course not, of course not, of course not. Please don't think that way. You were a wonderful husband, and I loved you and love you dearly. All of the flowers, the beautiful cards—most men would not keep that up, all thoughts from you for love to me. That is why we are talking now.

Wednesday Morning, March 2

[That monkey face I saw in my dream last night—was that you?]

Of course not. Think of me as the way you knew me in my physical body. I know you thought I was sexy and pretty. I guess I was, and actually, in your mind's eye, I'm still pretty.

[I miss you so much.]

I wish you wouldn't, as I am fine. More than fine. I am happy, joyful, and love you. Please live your life now to the fullest. Please, please. I will always be with you if you want me to be.

[But I can't see you—the full you.]

Yes, but you will some night and maybe day.

Friday Morning, March 4

[Hi. Are you okay?]

You know that I am. As you know, I am reading some of your feelings, and I am sorry that I over-controlled you sometimes in our life together.

[Don't concern yourself, as I also tried to control you sometimes. This is what happens in a marriage. We had a wonderful life together. I am amazed that I met you, loved you, and still do, and we lived our thirty-three-plus years together. We had a lot of fun, and I believed that you loved and still love me terribly. That enabled me to see love and find love myself. I adored you and still do.]

Please just relax, live in the now, and think of me as you want to. I left when I was ready, although I did not know it at the time. It has turned out to be the best for me. I was unhappy with my body situation, my looks, and my inability to take care of myself as I had always done. It really upset me. Thank you for all you did for me in my time of trial. Think of me, but live in the now, please. It's nice you are going to make an album of our life together. I also miss you physically. We can talk without your having to write.

Chapter 5

---◇◈◇◈◈◇---

THE BLUE JAY AND
OTHER PHENOMENA

Monday Morning, March 7, the Blue Jay

[On our back deck, which is off the rear kitchen entrance, Sue and I would often sit in the summer, read, and see blue jays drop down to the deck from a tree overlooking the deck to get peanuts that we would throw to them. We think the blue jay is a beautiful bird, predominantly blue with a white chest and blue underpants and a blue crest. It has a black U-shaped collar and a black border around its neck. It feeds on nuts and seeds. The males and females and small newborns that start to fly all drop down for peanuts. They sometimes swallow a whole unshelled, unsalted peanut in their gullet and hold one in their mouth as they fly away. This has happened for several years. They always come back. The summer of 2015, before Sue's operation, they seemed to come a little earlier. One large male blue jay took a liking to Sue, and when she was in the kitchen, it would scream at her from outside the closed sliding glass door for peanuts. Like, "Where are my peanuts?"

Sue had told me she was going to give me another sign that she was all right, happy, and joyful. Maybe sooner than later.

Last night, as I was going to sleep, I had a thought from her how I would like a sign. I told her that it really did not matter, but I would like to see her either as she was after the operation or the way she was dressed in a favorite photo of mine, wearing her lovely clothes and Indian turquoise jewelry, but I really did not care how the sign appeared.

In the middle of the night, I was awakened by a constant chirping coming from the left side of my bed. About halfway between the top of the bed and the ceiling, about seven feet to my left, I saw a blue jay with its wings folded, hanging in the air and constantly chirping. It was colored a faint blue, and the outside of the image was kind of fuzzy, like an improperly taken camera shot. I was wide awake, and my immediate reaction, which I said out loud, was, "The blue jays have returned."

Then it dawned on me: *How can a blue jay be in the bedroom in the middle of the night?* It continued chirping, and after a full seven or eight seconds, it was gone. I then realized that it was Sue showing me a sign that I would immediately recognize. I even said instinctively, "Sue, is that you?" She had told me she would give me a sign that she was all right, and she did. As you can imagine, that blew my mind. This, to me, is a fantastic phenomenon of imaging, as I have been reading in my research on after-death communications.]

[As I always say, I really miss you and our years together.]

I know. I miss you too. What did you think of the blue jay? I knew that you would think it was me, figuratively speaking. I am with you always, although you can't see me. I am glad that you are starting to relax and that you had the pictures made as a memory of my life on earth. As the minister said, I am now at rest where I am for a while after my journey on earth.

[Where are you? I keep asking since you are able to see through my eyes and perhaps hear and experience other senses through me.]

I am just out of your sight on a different vibration level where I feel joy, feel lightness, and have dropped the burdens of your physical earth. As you know, everything is vibration in the whole universe and beyond. I don't have all of the answers yet, as I am on a plane just outside of yours. I have no physical body but do not need one where I am. All of my needs, which are now almost none, are taken care of. This, where I am, is joy, light, happiness, carefree, and I am happy now.

No emotional problems, no physical problems, just enjoying the freedom and lightness of joy. What a relief after the trials and tribulations I had on earth. But please do not misunderstand that, as

I had a great (for the most part), pleasing journey on earth and deeply enjoyed our life together. It gave me pleasure and joy, although as you now know, I had some emotional problems. I still do not know why these happened, but nevertheless they did, and someday I will find out why my soul needed that journey.

There are many levels of vibration, leading up to and through spirit guides, angels, and finally a closeness, and, for lack of a better term, walk hand in hand with God. As the movie said, "Do not forsake me, my darling." I am well, and we will talk periodically. The more joyful you are, the higher vibrations we have together.

Tuesday Morning, March 8

[Hello.]

I am glad you are starting to slow down and are getting more sleep. I know that this has been quite a shock to you, coming so suddenly and without warning. I know that the blue jay figure really showed you that I remembered and that I am all right. That is why I showed myself as a blue jay, as I knew that not only would get your attention but would strike home again that I am me and joyful and happy in my new situation. We had a good time together and maybe will again. I am not that far along yet to know what the future holds, although there will not be any more dark days in my life. I did my time on earth and, for the most part, enjoyed it.

I learned to love unconditionally with your love and attention and help. I know that we both learned to love by being together and taking care of each other. I know you can't help being sad sometimes about me leaving you, but maybe some sadness is a good thing to help you with your good memories of us together. We had some great times among some minor problems, like a couple has. We kept our own identities and then merged some also.

I know that this is a lonely time for you sometimes, but it will get better, as you will keep some fond memories of our togetherness.

[It is unbelievable that you are gone.]

I know, but remember my passing from earth was a good thing for me after the illness problems I had. I can't tell you how happy and joyful I am now. If you could really understand that, you would be happy for me too. I know that blue jay situation finally made you realize that I am okay, that should relax your stress. I know it will; that is why I chose that method of coming to you so that you would really understand that I am fine.

As we go along and I develop where I am and where I am going from here, your knowledge of my situation will grow stronger and stronger. I love you. Good-bye for now so you can continue your day. We will communicate during the day from time to time, as we have been doing all along.

[Thank you again for showing me the blue jay. That really, really made me believe that you are all right, happy, and joyful where you are, wherever you are. What happened in the hospital room after you passed on?]

After I was pronounced clinically dead in the hospital room, I felt calmness for a few minutes and knew you came in to see me and kissed my forehead. I was calm, in no pain or discomfort. I really realized more than ever how much you really loved me. After a few short minutes, I left my body altogether and drifted upward toward a light. I just dissolved from my body and left, again as I say, into the bright dazzling light.

I was aware of myself, who I was, and felt unlimited joy. I drifted for a while like on a cloud and then was deposited in another world, a world without form as you know it. I am still resting, and I feel like I am relaxing after my earth journey. We will see what comes next, but I know it will be joyous and thrilling. Very important, the vibrations of love between us are keeping us together.

Thursday Morning, March 10

[Hi. You wanted to talk to me.]

Yes, I wish you wouldn't be so full of sorrow. I came to you as the blue jay so that you would recognize that only you and I would know that was a sign from me that I am well and fine. I am in another world—dimension, whatever you want to call it; heaven, if that word makes sense to you. Again, I am all right. I want you to live your life in happiness, not sorrow. We had a great time together, and think of that with joy. I am here with you, so please don't be so unhappy. Live your life, and do what you want to do. Relax and get some sleep.

I will come again to show you I am okay, so please, please think of me and our life together, but do not keep getting emotional over what has just happened. I love you so much, perhaps even more than when I was with you physically, now that I realize the sacrifices you made to help me.

Friday Morning, March 11

My Spirit Guides want to talk with you.

Spirit Guides:[She is in a vacuum right now between heaven and what you call earth. It is part of the universe. She is happy, well, joyful but misses you as well. She can miss you and still feel overall joy. She is happy out of her earthly body now, which was a joy for her until she became sick and felt sick for several years. She kept a lot of her sick feelings from you so that you would not worry about her.

Her spirit will be around for quite a while, as there is no time where she is now. She can communicate with us, and she wishes you well and to take better care of yourself. You really should not have any emotional sadness because she knows who she is and is not dead, as you call it. After a while she will graduate to a higher plane and will be able to talk with the angels that are close to God—Infinite Intelligence, as you call it.

Please don't ask us questions about who God is or where God is because we are not able to explain it to you in terms you mortals can understand. There is a hierarchy after transition that one must go through in joy to reach angel status. I know that this does not mean anything to you in your terms, but someday the consciousness of your people will more than really understand that. Sue will be able to communicate with you in all of her travels if you keep the lines of communication open with love vibrations.

[Will I meet her and know her someday when I transition?]

Yes, if you both want to; it is a mutual thing, but if you are both in communication through love vibrations, yes. She will help you through your transition. The departed from your earth will communicate with those whose vibrations are similar. There is no sadness or repercussions on anyone's part. You will think of her often but with fond memories of your life together. She wishes that you would not be sad because she had a good life with you, better than she knew with anyone else. She would like for you to think of her often but not with sadness.

Just be thankful that you had over thirty-three years together. I know now that you think that they went by in a second. You will find joy if you look for it. Good-bye for now.]

Please get some rest now, and we will talk later.
Sue

[*Note: A typical spirit guide has a purpose, and that purpose is to guide and teach you along a certain path. They often are beings that have led a physical life and have moved on to a spiritual life.*]

[I was thinking about our connection. Will it last?]

It will last as long as you want it to. I will not break the connection, as I don't want to. Love is the connection; that is, love vibrations between us. I don't want to and will not. Only you can break the connection if you want to. You have your life to live, and you do not know yet where your life will take you, so don't worry about breaking the connection. I will not, and as we have love between us, I cannot break the connection. I am glad that emotionally you are realizing that I am all right and are giving up all of the emotional grief that you are having. It is no longer necessary for you. You will have our memories of our physical life together, and that is good.

I am glad you are saving some of my things, as they will give you some emotional relief. I am glad that you are now starting to relax and work again and are looking to God—Universal Intelligence, whatever you call our unearthly situation. By unearthly, I mean not of this earth, the world you are now in. There is an Intelligent scheme of things that controls everything, which we call God, for lack of a better word or understanding.

I am just now starting to adjust to where I am. I feel like I am floating on a sea of clouds for now, happy, joyful, full of light. Where I will end up, I don't know, except I know it will be wonderful.

There are other happy, joyful spirits all around me, and they are people that have recently passed. We are all in a wonderful, fulfilling limbo but know that we will move up in the hierarchy of things— angels, et cetera. By et cetera, I mean closer to God. Everyone knows and remembers who they were on earth and can communicate with their loved ones, if the loved ones or unloved ones want them to. That is the key. We do not go where we are not invited.

Think of me as I was on earth with you, as that is the way I feel. I keep saying I love you, and I do, tremendously much, so I don't want you to think that I am being overly emotional in my thoughts of you. I can't be overly emotional; that is no longer necessary for me. For now, know that I am here for you whenever you want me to be. I am not going anywhere. (Pun.) I still have a good sense of humor.

Please go about your business, and, as you know, we can talk silently to each other all during the day when you are not distracted by your day-to-day living. I do not want to and cannot interfere with that. Have a good day.

Sue

It was nice for the doctor to call you yesterday. He is a good man, really liked us, and is sad himself for losing me. We cannot explain our situation. Most people, even learned people, will not believe in a future time after death now, but as the consciousness of the people on earth increases, they will come to realize that. Please think of me in any phase of our life together, as I am all that, whatever you think about. I am whatever age in your memory you want me to be when we talk. Good-bye for now. You have to get along with your day.

Saturday Morning, March 12

I want you to work as necessary, in a relaxed manner, to keep the house. I love our house, our home, and would like you to stay in it for as many years as you wish. If you have to sell my Jaguar to do that, it is okay. Obviously I do not need it anymore. I loved it while I had it, even though I could not drive it myself in the last couple of years. Do what you want with my clothes. I loved them while I was alive on earth, but now just do what you think best. I am glad that you realize that I am still with you, and we can communicate. You will be much happier now.

I don't have to give you any more signs that I am okay but will if you want, from time to time.

[Please do.]

Okay, will do. Busy day for you. See you.

Love,

Sue

Tuesday Morning, March 15

Why are you so down? You have seemed to feel better.

[I'm just tired with the daylight time change.]

You will be all right. I am here for you. You mentioned that you wished that we had gone to Hawaii again. Actually, you can go whenever you want, and I will be with you. I could go at any time, but it would not be fun without you. I can go anywhere in the universe now— actually anywhere in any universe—that I want to. I am a free spirit now but know who I am.

You were thinking about where I am. I am not in a parallel universe, or I could not be with you. I am just in another dimension but one without form as you know it. Just free-floating with love and joy. Please don't be alarmed if you don't see me for a while. You need to get along with your life, but I am always with you, and as time goes on, I will show myself to you, probably at night when your mind is clear from your day.

I could come at anytime, but it is obviously a time of my choosing. I am glad you are, in general, feeling better now, as some time has passed. You are getting some sleep and looking better. I did have a time of it this last year, but it has really worked out for the best for both of us. I love you, love you, love you. You are my knight in shining armor.

[Very frequently on a Sunday afternoon or evening, Sue and I would eat dinner at our favorite lobster restaurant. On this past Sunday night I decided to have dinner there and sat in a booth, as Sue and I used to do. I was reading while I was waiting to be served dinner. All of a sudden, I noticed a brightening and dimming on the pages of my book. In looking up, I noticed that the little ceiling spotlight above my booth started shining brighter and then blinking on and off. I looked at the other ceiling lights, and they were all lighted like normal.

There was no flashing, and they were all of the same kind of dim light that you see in a restaurant at night for mood lighting. I knew it was Sue again, playing with the electricity. One of the ways I can tell her signs is that all of a sudden I get goose bumps—vibrations all up and down my body. After a few minutes, the light returned to normal.]

[Sue, was that you again?]

Yes, that was me. It is a lot of fun for me, showing you that I am still here for you. Look for some other happenings from me, just so we can have some fun together. Go about your work now, if you will. Love you.

Sue

Chapter 6

---❖❖❖❖---

COMPUTER MANIPULATIONS

Wednesday Morning, March 16, The Credit Card

[One of the books I just bought suggests contacting your departed one by imagining a flight of stairs going up to a door that opens up into a garden. Imagine your loved one sitting on a bench in the garden. You sit next to him or her on the bench and visualize in your mind's eye putting your arm around his or her shoulders, like you perhaps did in real life. The book goes on to say you might have to do this for seven days in a row to be able to make the connection and actually feel your loved one physically; for example, touching your cheek.]

Hi. You tried to hold me like the book says. You saw a little faint light in your mind, saw the light moving up, the door opened, you went through it, in your mind's eye sat with me on the bench. I felt your arms around me. It was faint but remarkable on your first try. We will see what happens in the future if you want. I had to go, and you went back through the door. When you immediately tried to open the imaginary door again, it would not stay open. It is interesting for both of us.

[I was still searching the computer for more information on after-death communications. I found a couple more books that looked interesting. I tried to buy one, but my credit card would not go through, although the credit card was good. I tried it three times, and all three times it was rejected. So then I immediately tried the other book, and the credit card went right through.]

The book you bought was the one I wanted you to buy. As you

41

know, when over the Internet you tried to buy the wrong one, the credit card would not go through, and you tried it three times. It would have been the wrong book. That made you go back, see the other book I wanted you to buy, and the credit card immediately went through. This book now tells you exactly what happened to you—the lights flickering, about things like the blue jay can happen. It is remarkable how that reinforced your views and solidified the things that happened to you before you ever had the book. Hooray!

Wednesday Morning, March 16

[I miss you terribly, even though I know you are all right.]

I know, but I am in the other room because my pictures are in the other room, and when you go to see them, I am there. You cannot see me, but I am there with you; that is how strong our similar vibrations are.

[When I looked at one of the photos the other night, her eyes seemed to be staring at me with an intensity that I didn't remember in the photograph.]

The other night you saw that my eyes seemed to be staring at you. Don't be alarmed, but I want you to know you are not alone. By the way, I did not die alone. I knew you were there, and that was sweet when you kissed me on the forehead. I was not completely gone, although it seemed to you and everyone that I was gone. However, after you kissed my forehead, I knew everything would be all right, and so I completely left immediately.

[Note: The books that I purchased and scientific information that I found after all of these things started to happen are listed in the back of this book. It is interesting that many of the people who were brain dead for a few minutes and then came back (near-death experience) have mentioned their consciousness remained for a while. This enforces my belief that consciousness will continue even for the ones that continue on to heaven.]

Thursday Morning, March 17

[Hi.]

Hi. I am glad you are starting to feel better and happy now. It has been a long, tough road for you the last six weeks. I love you, and you know it, and that has helped keep you going. You must live your life in the now and realize I will always be here with you when you listen for me. Don't ask me the tough questions you have now about where I am and what I am doing. You and all on earth can't conceive of the plane I am now on. Just realize I am here for you and will always be. Read the book again; you will get more out of it, and you will feel even better.

Take your time about cleaning and fixing the house. Everything will be all right with it. I know you are worrying about it and the money in this market, but realize that you are just starting to work again after my departure and the many months of taking care of me, taking beautiful care of me. I love you, and I am going to let you go now so you can go back to work. Suz

Friday Morning, March 18, The Computer

[You wanted me to write about my computer experience yesterday afternoon.]

Yes.

[I was working on a business program on the computer when the monitor screen went blank. I tried the program again, and it would not come up. Sue had told me how easy it was for the departed to manipulate electricity, radios, TVs, computers, and other electromagnetic devices. This also is discussed in the materials in the back of the book.

All of a sudden, the screen filled with a program that I had forgotten I'd purchased several years ago and did not remember it was still in the computer. It was a three-page program titled "My New Self-Image" that came up one page at a time so I could print them out. Immediately after that, an old color photograph of me came up on a separate page, one that was in another section of the computer. Sue was concerned about my self-esteem and not only pulled up the self-esteem program but also brought up a photograph of me to show me that this was something that I should read and use. I was dumbfounded. It was completely beyond my understanding. As soon as this was printed out, the business program I was working on reappeared.]

[Last night I awakened in the middle of the night and felt a soft breeze on the right side of my cheek. This came and went for about five seconds. I had never felt a cool breeze before in the bedroom, as we never opened a window. It had to be you coming through to me for some reason.]

Yes, that was me. I cannot reach out to you during the day yet. I say *yet*, but I'm able to come through at night. Much easier for me to lower my vibrations to meet yours when your brain activity is at a minimum.

Sue

Friday Night, March 18

[Where are you?]

You know I am on a different plane, but to answer your question, I am happy, joyful, and have loving guardian angels around me. I did not have any pain when I passed over. It was like a great white light descended on me, and it was pure joy. I know who I am, and I know everything that happened in my life on earth and with you. I feel our love—hope you can keep it. Loved you and still do, unconditionally. You really took great care of me, keeping a roof over our heads. We had moments but few and far between, and many of them were my fault because of some anger I always had deep inside from before I met you.

I know you still have fear that I will leave you, but fear not. I won't unless you want me to. I am very close to you, closer than you realize. I wish you would relax about this. When you pass on, I will be here and come to receive you with love. So don't worry, as you know there is no death, as we have been taught all along that death was final. Not so, as you know from many of my experiences with you.

I am glad that you found our scrapbook. I know that means a lot to you and me too that you have it. You can add the pictures to the new book you bought. Just think of me as if I am in another room. I am sorry I left you with so much junk in my office, but as you know, the last year I just did not have the energy to go through and toss out what I did not need.

Sue

[How close are you to God?]

Very close, God's light and soul are nearby and cover me with love. It is hard to explain to you on earth, but it is a flowing love that never ceases. It is like being in a warm shower of love instead of water all of the time. I don't know where I go from here, but my guardian angel will be with me as well as my spirit guides. I am assured that I can talk with you forever and feel our love forever. I have not found out about reincarnation or even if there is a thing of reincarnation, like so many gurus on earth think there is. Many of the stories of reincarnation came from hypnosis, and in the case you mentioned, maybe the people hypnotized wanted to give the hypnotist a story that they thought he or she wanted. You would think that if there were such a thing that I would have heard about it by now. All in good time. I just want to relax after my time on earth and not get into any deep stuff. I hate the word *stuff*, but that is your vocabulary, not mine.

Saturday Morning, March 19

[Do you mind my asking what kind of a body, if any, you now have, since you were so beautiful when you were here?]

No, I don't mind your asking. I have kind of a celestial body; that is, a feeling of being surrounded by light—a bright, beautiful light, sparkling light. A joyful feeling with all of my cares I had on earth dissolved, and I am at peace. My body in your terms—think of it as a bright, beautiful twinkling star. That probably is as close of an analogy as I can relate so that you can understand. But I am me that you always knew and loved.

I am very close to you. You know, don't you? By close I don't mean

45

from a body standpoint but from a mental and emotional standpoint. Yes, we have emotions, or we would not exist ourselves. That is very important because what else is unconditional love except emotion? Have a very good day and will talk to you later, as you need to get along with your day.

Suz

Monday Morning, March 21

[What is happening to you?]

Not much. I am still resting; however, I am awaiting the next step in my growth. I am surrounded by what you would call angels, although that really is not an apt description of these heavenly beings. I know you were thinking that this situation has completely changed your thinking about your life, God, and your journey that you still have on earth.

Now that you understand all that has happened, you will never really be the same in your thinking about your present life on earth. For all of your life and mine, we thought that just living with all of the joys, trials, and tribulations was all there is, even if we thought about it at all during our daily living and pursuits of our desires, goals, and wishes.

As you drive your car down the streets, eat, or sleep, you have a new concept of life on earth. All of the people you see that go about their lives feel that everything is concrete; the sky is blue; the homes they live in, the cars and material things they own, their work, their entire lives are so "down-to-earth," so to speak, that they cannot and probably do not consider that there is a larger picture that you and I know and acknowledge now. In our new perspective and knowledge, it is difficult to put into words the way we used to feel, like most everyone now feels, about life.

You had asked me who else I saw or felt as I was transferring out of my physical body. I felt and saw my father who passed before, lots of friends that I previously had that had moved on, but there was love— but not the feeling of unconditional love like you and I have for one another. Again, as I mentioned, I left the hospital room even as the doctors had given up and I was clinically dead. I remained without pain for a few moments, even minutes, and felt and saw in my mind you standing there, gingerly kissing my forehead, and I could feel the nurse outside in the hall, really upset and crying and giving you a hug. You all, of course, did not know this, and I then completely left.

As I told you this morning, I want you to stop thinking of what could have happened, what you could have done differently to save me at home. I know this is a very common reaction, but under our circumstances now, it is very self-defeating and emotionally exhausting. I am saying this with love, but please stop going there, as I am now happy and joyful, and you really know it.

So why continue to be sorry and sad over what all along has been the very best, under the circumstances? I might have had years as a prisoner of my own imperfect body. God does things in his own loving way and in his own time, and that was now for me.

Again Monday Morning, March 21, Talking Picture Frame

[I have a battery-operated talking picture frame that Sue gave me several years ago as a present. The photo is of her standing next to the Jaguar automobile. I keep that next to some of her photographs on the dining room bureau. For two nights now, I have picked up her pictures and the talking picture frame has been activated. I was close to the frame but the activation button was at the far end that I was not touching. I do get goose bumps just thinking about it.]

Tuesday Morning, March 22

[Hello.]

Hello, good morning. I like you. Do you have a question?

[Without being redundant, I am still confused about how close you are, and can you be everywhere at once?]

Yes, on my plane, I can be close to you and know what you are doing at all times, and whenever you want, you can tune in to me, as I do not and cannot interfere with your thoughts, your life, and your free will. I can be elsewhere too at the same time, since I understand that there will be no limits on my freedom to float wherever I want in this universe or any other universe.

[What about other universes?]

That is still a little mystery to me, still being grounded in our known universe. I will find out and be shown in good time; however, there is no time here. That is just your earthly saying, about time. I understand that there are many universes stretching into infinity and continuing to enlarge. This is the Universal Spirit's work, which we, for a lack of understanding, call God.

God is just an earthly term for this Intelligent Universal Spirit. I mean no harm in what I just said. If the word God reflects your understanding, great. Many people on earth use the term God, Universal Spirit, Great One, Supreme Intelligence—it makes no difference; all of the words are interchangeable. Just know that there is a Universal Loving Intelligence that creates all. I can't explain it yet. I just feel it, and my angels and spirit guides are teaching me—will start teaching me—all of these things. The main thing is that everything is pure love, and along with that comes unbelievable feelings of joy.

I know you want a more definite answer, but I can't give it to you now. Maybe someday in the future. But the thing that I want to get across to you again and again is that I love you and want the best for you. Do not concern yourself about me because I am happier than I ever was on earth, although I loved my life, for the most part, and remember with pleasure our life together, which was beautiful.

I am glad that I had all of my experiences, good and bad; had fun, for the most part; loved my physical body most of my life, until the last couple of years when I was becoming more ill. God has his own ways, and we cannot fathom what our souls need; only God knows. I know this is all a mystery to you, but that is as it should be now. Don't strain your mind to try to understand that which is not understandable for you, at least in this point in time.

[This still seems strange to communicate like this when I cannot see you or be with you.]

Just feel like you are talking with me by telephone, if that seems to make it better for you.

[Will I see you again in the near future? I would at least like to see some symbols from you.]

Maybe, I can't promise, as my vibrations have to be in congruence with yours, but probably. I came over as the blue jay, and I can probably do something like that again. Maybe I can project to you a picture of some type, like a body appearing clothed in some way, kind of like the picture you have of me. We will see.

Love,

Suz

Vaulted ceiling floodlights that were flashing 2 and 3
nights after Sue's passing

Area at the foot of the bed where most of happenings at night occured

Program that appeared on the monitor screen out of the depths of the computer

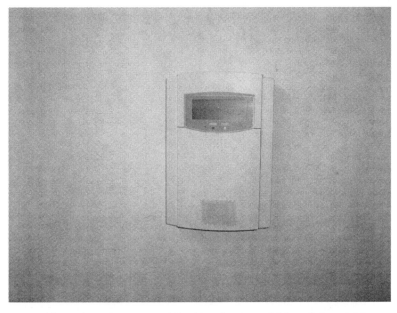

Alarm box that started flashing in the middle of the night

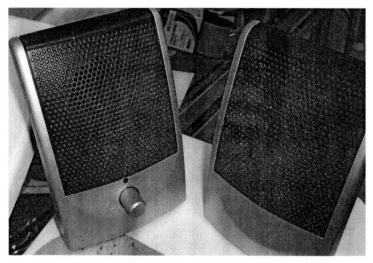

Speaker lights that were flashing in the middle of the night

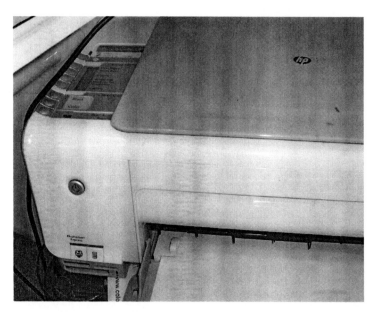

Printer light that started flashing in the middle of the night

Chapter 7

MUSIC MESSAGES

Wednesday Morning, March 23, Cell Phone Music

[Earlier this morning as I was driving out of our residential subdivision I had my cell phone turned on as I always do. As I approached the exit to the street, all of a sudden my cell phone started playing music. I have never tried to play any kind of songs on my phone and I have never learned how as I only use it for business. I pulled over and wrote down the words although they were coming through faster than I could write them down.

It was a man's voice and the words and different songs in order had lyrics as follows. "Will you be lonely tonight, I will come back to you, I will never leave you, Comeback to me, Why did you leave me, I will miss you" and other lyrics that I could not catch.,

I asked Sue how she did it and she told me it was simple. I just go" into the either", her term not mine, find the music I want and I just play it on your cell phone. Kind of like I created the flashing lights in the dining room the second and third nights of my transition.]

[*Note: The dictionary defines* ether *as a rarefied element believed to fill the upper regions of space, upper region of space/heavens; also, a wave theory of light permeates all space and transmits transverse waves.*]

Thursday Morning, March 24

[I just do not know where you are.]

I know that. It is just impossible for you, in your human condition, to comprehend this situation, but it is real for me. I am me, my spirit is me, and my soul is me. Where I go from here I do not know yet, but I know that it will be in a wonderful place because I am so full of peace, love, and joy, and my God is a loving entity. Please don't worry and concern yourself, as we will stay in touch, and you will see. I am glad you are writing the book and typing it yourself to save money.

[What's next?]

I don't know. Let's just play it by ear and see what comes up. I know you were going through my notes of the past years as you were cleaning up my office. I am glad you did, as you saw many good and bad aspects of my life you really did not know. However, I really did not have any bad aspects except for my health problems that came and went.

Sometimes I felt really healthy, although at other times I felt emotionally down. It was kind of a roller-coaster ride, but all in all, I was terribly happy, and happy being with you, doing the things we did together. It was really fun and the only way I wanted to live after we met. We had wonderful times together, and be assured this is not the end. We will be together again—at least our spirits and our knowledge of each other and closeness of each other in an afterlife. I know from your perspective now that seems strange, but it will happen.

Friday Morning, March 25, Phone Ring

[Last night I was awakened out of a deep sleep by a loud telephone ring from the area in the bedroom where we kept our land-line telephone, but the telephone was not there, as I removed it sometime ago.]

I wanted to talk about last night. You were sound asleep, and I thought I could materialize to the point you could see some of me. That is why I woke you up with the loud telephone ring, from that area where the vibrations still were. It was easier for me to do them from there.

Actually, I tried to materialize and did a little bit at the foot of your bed by the picture on the wall of the women dropping their earthly baggage before they started moving off to heaven. Actually, I did materialize a little bit, but I could not get my vibrations low enough to completely materialize, even for a fraction of a second.

I understand that you could not really see anything, but after you got up to get a glass of water, you noticed your upper bed sheet full of sparkling electrical flashes. That was some energy that I had left over, and the only way I could show you was through the flashes on the upper bed sheet as you got back into bed. That was the only fabric in the room that you would notice that would capture some of my energy.

I will try another night sometime to materialize so that you will know that it is me, but I have to learn how to get my vibrations down to kind of being in contact with yours. You have a lot to do today, so I will let you go. Thank you for taking the time to write this because I know you are in a hurry.

Talk to you again soon.

Sue

Saturday Morning, March 26

Hi. Do you have any questions?

[Not really. Do you have anything to tell me?]

Yes. Have a nice Easter. I am glad you bought a lily that you can bring home and think of me because you know how much I love flowers. Please do not be sad tomorrow on Easter. I wish you would not go deeply into the emotional past because the past is past. I know you will always think of me on earth with you, great loving memories, but please do not dwell on them to the point of sadness. They should come across as happy memories. It is too easy for people to dwell on the past and be sad all of the time.

You now have a life to live. Think of me. Talk to me like we are doing, but please don't dwell on sadness. When you think of the past, I want you to feel happy. Increase your vibrations of joy and live a joyful life. You are strong, and I know you can do that, so think of me if you want to, but please do not fret over what happened.

It was God's will that I left when I did because I was really concerned about my being able to make a living after you were gone since you are fifteen years older than I was. My mother would be gone, and maybe my brother would be gone. We didn't have any children because I did not really want any at my age when we got married.

I could have ended up in deep trouble since I was concerned about ever getting my stamina and health back after the operation. I would not have wanted to live my life dependent on other people who did not know me in my prime, who might not have given me the best of care. I would have continued on for many years by myself, lonely and in some back ward of a county nursing home.

Again, I am happy, joyful, lightly spirited, blessed, and close to my angels and spirit guides. I am no longer concerned about my future, as it will be a blessed one. You cannot believe how joyful I am, and I am a free spirit.

Love,

Sue

Be happy for me.

Sunday Morning, March 27, Bicycle Horn Honk

[Last night in the middle of the night, I was abruptly awakened by a loud honk on the bicycle horn that I had attached to Sue's hospital bed. This was a great idea for her to awaken me in the night when she needed help going to the bathroom. This worked beautifully while she was alive. The horn was detached from her bed after she was gone, as I took several items she loved and boxed them for safe keeping for a while—some new clothing that were Christmas presents, a couple of sweatshirts with lovely painted scenes, her new tennis shoes, a cute little stuffed bunny rabbit, and the bicycle horn. I left the box in a corner of the bedroom. The horn sound did not come from the area of the box. It came from across the room by her bed, where there was no horn.]

Hi, I still really could not materialize last night but I will. I honked the horn, though. Ever since you took the horn off of the bed, the vibrations of the bicycle horn that I used at night to awaken you when I needed to go to the bathroom were still in the area of my bed, just like the telephone vibrations were still in the area where the phone used to be.

Interesting, isn't it? I don't know how long the vibrations will last or really why they are still there, but I can use them whenever I need to awaken you to see what we can do on my materialization. You might have seen a faint light on the wall at the foot of the bed near the angel picture on the wall. I like that picture and probably will use that area when I can.

I really do not want to be redundant, but I am glad you are now really starting to take care of yourself and have started to gain some weight.

[On this business about the phone ring and the horn honk and the other inexplicable things that you have been doing—how do you do it?]

It is really hard for me to explain it to you, but your vibrations on planet earth are so low, it is easy for me to control them in a loving, vibrational way because if my vibrations were not so high in love—love vibrations control everything since God is love—it would not happen.

Any lower vibrations than love vibrations will not work. That is why, unfortunately, many people cannot receive because there is not, in general, with obvious exceptions, very much love at this time on earth. Too much discrimination, too many war vibrations, too much hate or dislike among groups, and there are many evil intentions. If I had any lower than love vibrations I could not come through to you, or anything I would like to do to help you or show you that I am all right would not, could not happen. Hope that helps. Talk to you again.

Suz

I am glad you are starting to enjoy life again.

Monday Morning, March 28, E-mail Sound

[I was awakened by an e-mail sound in the bedroom.]

Hi, I tried to manifest last night, as you know, but our vibrations did not match. I awakened you with an e-mail sound, as if a new e-mail was coming across your computer you have downstairs in your office when you have it turned on. It is easy for me to make an electronic sound. In order for me to manifest for you, I need to lower my vibrations more, which I can do, but you need to bring yours up more.

If you could now find joy or even not be sad as much or just feel good with gratitude for what you have, as much as possible, your vibrations would come up, and I would be able to manifest to the degree you will know it is me. We will see. Anyhow, it is not a necessary thing anyway. As you know, I am fine, but it would be nice for you. Enjoy your day.

Love,

Suz

Tuesday Morning, March 29

[Some of the books I am now reading talk about when they have a death experience and come back to life, they have seen golden light, shining light, angels, and beautiful surroundings. Is that what happened to you, and do you want to talk about it?]

Yes, actually, not only did that happen—beautiful, shining, brilliant light surrounding me—but being surrounded by lovely music along with joyful angels and other souls that had passed before, all welcoming me into what you call heaven. It is impossible for you to understand what happens. You cannot comprehend the majesty and shining beauty of the afterlife. Think of the finest opera you have ever seen and multiply that a thousand fold, and you will be able to try and see what is going on with me.

Just realize I am joyful and feel unconditional love all around me. Still, I know exactly who I am and have all of the same qualities about me now that I had on earth when you knew me. I am me, the one you loved. You have a big day. Please go about your day, and we talk again soon. All of my love and affection. More shortly.

Sue

Wednesday Morning, March 30

Hi. The body has a brain with nerves, which control the workings of muscles; the ability to interpret information sent to the brain by eyes, ears, and other sensory organs; as well as many other functions that are gone when a person passes away, but you are still you. Obviously, the personality must go to the afterlife since I am still me. The personality and the spirit are inseparable and completely separate from the physical brain. I am me, the same person you knew on earth.

So the brain operates the physical body, the heart pumping, the lungs breathing, the body moving, the cells working. In other words, the physical you, as you know you, is all handled by the brain. The brain is akin to a computer in that it operates the physical body, just as a computer does not as yet have emotions, a distinctive personality, or any feelings, hopes and dreams, the brain just operates as a complex motor, if you will. The me that you knew—and I should say, still know—has not changed in my transition. Hope that all makes sense.

I have just discarded my shell that I needed to live on earth, but not my spirit, my personality, the me that I have been and always will be. To change the subject, I wish you would not think of me when I was in the hospital in the ICU before I passed, with all of the doctors and nurses working on me that made you very sad. That situation is all over and long gone. Think of me anyway you want while we were together, and those will be happy, joyful memories. This will enable you to carry on your life with joy and happiness. So eliminate the sadness.

You know very well from everything that has happened since I left that I am fine, me, happy. I like the expression "dancing with the stars." You know I am with you constantly, every time you want me to be, and loving you, so please, please think of me, but move on from sadness to joy, and enjoy the rest of your life. Actually, you know that I can see through your eyes, know what you are doing, and give you help and suggestions, but I cannot interfere with your intentions because God has given you free will to live your life as you so desire, so that your soul can grow and expand.

[What about the soul?]

The soul is separate from the spirit. The soul is on a much higher plane, close to God—or if you prefer, Higher or Creative Intelligence, All-Knowing Spirit. It does not matter the name you put on the Creator of the universe, or should I say universes, and knows God completely.

[How close are you to God? Do you want to discuss that?]

Yes. It is hard to explain to you, but I will try. When I died—I know you don't like that word, but when I passed on, I felt like the sky opened up, like I was on a cloud but a brilliant gold cloud that kept rising and rising until I felt like I was in pure shining joy with other spirits all around me. Everything was brilliant, just indescribable happiness and joy. I left all of my earthly baggage behind and was floating on a cloud of love. God is love, and in that respect I am with God. No more fear, no more worry, just a light feeling, like being inside a star. It is indescribable shining beauty and precious love.

When you drive down a road and enter a cloud, the mists are around you, but you cannot really reach out and hold the cloud. It just is. Picture a gold, shiny cloud, without any concrete substance, just an unbridled sense of joy, unbelievable lightness of joy. That is what I believe God is, but with a beautiful intelligence—higher and brighter, unbelievable intelligence. I am not able to describe the feeling, just a complete sense of freedom, like floating on a cloud, having been unburdened of all cares, yet I know who I am.

As I progress in my journey, and it is a journey, I will know more about the unseen scope of the universe, but as I have mentioned, I can be everywhere at once. No time and no dimensions as you know them. I am just me, the complete essence of me, the complete me that I was on earth, except without the physical body.

I know that this is hard for you to understand and comprehend, but you do not have to. When you pass on, you know that you and I will be together, if that is what you still want. There is no loneliness, no lonely feeling, just everything is complete, and I am happier than I have ever been and thought I would ever be. I am complete.

Chapter 8

---✦✦✦---

MORE SIGHTINGS AND SIGNS

Friday Morning, April 1, More Activity

[Last night I was awakened from a dream about 1:30 a.m. I do not remember the dream, but I saw a woman standing in the bedroom doorway with her back to me, wearing a blouse and a skirt. She was framed by a doorway, looking out into a garden that had beautiful, lush, colorful flowers. Just a row of flowers on each side of a central green grassy area. Was that you?]

Yes, I wanted to show you that I was still here with you. I still have not developed the ability to have you look at me from the front. I really don't know why I am not doing that yet. Maybe it is going to be too much for you now at this early juncture, and you need to gradually accept the fact that I can come to you. Yes, that is it, now that I think about it. Also, I want you to start journaling about your emotions and thoughts and life.

That is why last night, when you turned on your computer, the first thing you saw were the pages showing how to journal that I wanted you to see. Now I just want you to relax and go about your daily life without too much thought about the past. Please don't keep thinking about the hospital scene. That is over and done with, and you must move on. I am alive where I am, gloriously happy and joyful, so please let go of your anguish about my having died on your plane. There is no point in rehashing what is over. Think about our memories together. That is okay, and I would like you to do that and remember our times together.

Sue

Saturday Morning, April 2, US Flag

[I am confused about where you are in relationship to heaven.]

There are several levels where I am. The first level after passing is now where I am. It is a resting time after life on earth. I am surrounded by angels and other people that I have known that have passed. I understand that I will go to another level after a while. There are seven levels before I reach God's level in heaven. It is a soul-growing period. Please compare it with grade school, high school, and university on earth. It is a growing experience for the soul.

The soul is learning all of the time and being taught by several levels of angels that are on each level. Obviously, it is hard for you to comprehend all of this. I will continue to have my spirit, to know who I am and remember my experience on earth. There is love, unconditional love that will follow me on each level. There is a permanent top level of heaven where God is. Everything is joy, unbelievable joy, which is Source energy.

As long as you have love for me, and unconditional love is by far the better, we will stay in touch on each level, and I can help you through the rest of your life and help you through your passing, which, as you know, is inevitable at some point in time in the next several years. Hopefully, you can enjoy many more years on earth in good health.

[Last night I was awakened by the sound of your bicycle horn that is still in the bedroom. The sound came from the area where it is stored in the box with some of your clothes. I was fully awake, and just for a second or two and I saw a US flag flying and rippling in the wind in bright colors toward the bottom of my bed. It was over on the left side about halfway between the floor and the ceiling, except there is no wind in the bedroom. It appeared to be about two feet by three feet. The time was 2:58 a.m. What does the flag mean?]

Not really any meaning. I just need some tools from time to time to show you that I am here so you will, hopefully, quit thinking about my passing. I know you are really starting to process my death and are much more relaxed about it and really starting to get involved with your life again.

Sunday Morning, April 3

[Hello. Do you want to tell me again what happened when you died?]

Yes, there was quiet at first. Then an angel appeared, shimmering in white and gold, kind of like a mist. Then my dad appeared, and both of them said they would help me over the threshold of death and into another world, a world without suffering like I went through. Then a kind of a door opened, hard to describe, and we went through it, and then there were a myriad of angels around me, showing me I was all right, and they welcomed me into their world. At first I was confused, as I had just left the only world I knew, earth, but as they welcomed me with shining light, a sense of joy and deep, deep all consuming love enveloped me, and I knew that I was all right and at home.

Then I was led into a room of shining color. There were fresh, unbelievable flowers around me and in front of me as I went into a chamber of unbelievable light and a feeling of love. I now felt like I was floating among stars, and I could move anywhere I wanted in the universe. I can come back to you as I have done and help you in your life by giving you suggestions and guidance, like the angels did for me while I was on earth. I now feel guided again by the angels of God to more beautiful areas of heaven. I don't know where I will end up, but it will be in a wondrous spot in heaven, where my soul will continue to grow and learn about even more love and eventually be with God.

It is difficult to explain all of this in terms you can understand. All I want you to know now is that I am me. I am full of exquisite joy. I feel light and free and am happy. I can glide back into your field of love vibrations and again, through our love, help you on your way through life. I can feel that you are concerned about my going away, but as long as we have our love vibrations I will be here for you. I do not foresee changing because my love for you will not change or go away. Does that help?

Again, my darling, see you later. I know you don't use the word *darling*, but I like to say it now. More later.

[Note: As I mentioned early on, some of the wording may seem redundant, but I want to keep it the way it has come through to me on a day-to-day basis.]

Monday Morning, April 4

[Some of the books I am now reading say that in the other realm your soul continues to grow through your study and learning. What can you tell me about that, if you want to? What do you learn?]

Yes, it is a growth-and-expansion period of getting deeper into love and exploring the many mysteries of the universe. It is learning, almost like earth school, about the complexity of God. There are so many facets of the face of God that it is difficult to understand everything all at once. Obviously, we are not studying like we did. There is no verbal communication, no spelling, no written word, no learning of the earth's history, but there is learning for us of deeper emotional issues—but not negative emotional issues because there are none.

[What is this leading up to?]

It is leading up to a deeper meaning of all spiritual things, a deeper meaning of God and the universes. Realize that when we cross over, we are in the lower realms, if you will, of heaven, and our souls need to expand to climb to the higher levels, where there is pure love and joy. Hope that kind of makes sense.

[What about the evaluation of your life on earth? Does that happen, and if so, when?]

I guess that can happen just as soon as the spirit and soul leave the body. That did not happen for me, as I had lived a good life with love and faith for humanity. Probably if there was a situation where someone was evil, like deliberately killing somebody or whatever else, that person would have to go through an examination of where he goes next for learning.

Hope that answers your question. Please keep your vibrations up, as I would like to be close to you, as you actually see a vision of me.

Thanks.

Love,

Sue

I would like to add that part of the learning is to grow in wisdom and expand my soul even more than it is now.

Tuesday Morning, April 5, Water Bottle

[I am tired, but I feel pretty good. This is going to be a good day.]

I know it will be for you. Just relax and take it easy, and get your strength back up.

[When I opened the garage door yesterday morning, there was a little snowbank on the concrete driveway. Right next to the snowbank was a new bottle of water, a brand I do not buy, unopened, just laying there outside the garage door. It was even cooled by the snow. I thought at the time, *Where in the world did this come from?* We live deep in a cul-de-sac. It had no dust on it and was a good store brand name.

The books I am now reading talk about objects from loved ones appearing as a method of showing that they are still alive in another world. One was a white feather on a car windshield wiper, like the one the author's boyfriend wore in his hatband. Another one was a beautifully formed arrowhead like the woman's mother used to find on her walks in another town. It appeared while her daughter was on a hiking trail in a different state, where there was not supposed to be any arrowheads.

So the bottle of water must have been a gift from Sue, telling me I needed to drink more water, as I have been drinking too much tea and soda pop. At the least, it was a strange situation. Too many other things happen that cannot be attributed to coincidence, especially when Sue is telling me that she is going to continue to give me signs.]

Did you get the bottle of water the other day? I gave it to you because I want you to drink a lot more water for your health and much less tea. I am glad that you [really believe] in the afterlife and are developing a closeness to God. I know this has "completely thrown you for a loop," but it is what it is, and now you can live your life in a much different way. I know that you will live in a more humble, thankful way and start even more thinking of other human beings, their desires, and their needs and dreams. This whole situation has given you a 360-degree turnaround in your emotional thinking, and that is a good thing. You were always a thoughtful person, but this has given you a whole new way of thinking about life and has started you on a whole new chapter of your life which has yet to unfold.

Love,

Sue

Wednesday Morning, April 6, License Plate

[Yesterday I went to pick up my daughter at her house several miles away. As I drove into her housing complex driveway, a FedEx truck pulled in ahead of me, and the ending on the license plate was SUZ. Only four minutes later, another car came out of a garage near my daughter's house and drove by me, and the license plate ended in SUZ. In all of my years of travel in this state, I have never seen any license plates ending in SUZ, much less seeing two in a row within minutes of each other. But since it was a state-manufactured license plate, they obviously do use those letters on some plates, along with all of the other letters.

I have been interested, after all of these happenings, in finding as much as I can on happenings of this type from other sources. In another book I am reading, a person might have a passed love one show a sign that she or he is all right by showing their name on some item on a passing car, like a license plate or some other identifying item.]

[Sue, how did you do this?]

It is not that hard to position two vehicles like that. It is just a time sequence, and I can do that.

Thursday Morning, April 7

[There is so much to do. I am concerned about the real estate market. This is so strange. There are very few houses on the market, and those that are on the market are selling right away with people longing for houses. I didn't realize how much I leaned on you.]

We both leaned on each other. That is the way a good marriage should be when two people are close. You will be all right. God will look after you. Please lean on God, as He can handle it. Just take it one step at a time. Don't try to do everything at once like you have been trying to do. Remember I am with you and will help you. Even though I am in a different place, you can still lean on me to help you and give you emotional support; that is how it should be.

Again, take your time. Don't be sad, and realize that I am in a better place than I was on earth after my operation. Don't you hate that term "in a better place"? Everyone uses that to console, but it is true. Relax. I am with you.

Love,

Suz

Friday Afternoon, April 8

[Last night in the middle of the night I was abruptly awakened by a loud gun shot in the bedroom. The bedroom was dark but the top of the tall chest of drawers toward the left and about three feet from the bottom of the bed was briefly illuminated and I saw a cowboy hat that was apparently sitting on top fall down toward the floor. I turned on the light to get out of bed to see that portion of the floor and there was no hat on the floor. I do not own a cowboy hat. Sue was again showing me that she was alive and well in Heaven.]

[How did you do this again?]

You asked last night for another sign so I gave you one. It is kind of fun for me.

Love you to death. Pun.

Suz

Tuesday Morning, April 12, Spirit Guides

[All of the happenings—like the lights flashing, songs, blue jay materializing, bicycle horn noise—are wondrous, but how are they done by vibrations?]

[Spirit Guides came through to talk to me.]

Spirit Guides:[Well, as she says, it is very difficult for you as a human being to understand any of this. She is away from your planet. It is like a huge cloud, practically the size of your universe. Think of it as a cloud, which it certainly is not, but think of it as a gigantic, very luminous, much less dense floating cloud that is almost a universe in itself where every soul and spirit of each human that has passed resides.

Like Sue, a spirit—let's call it that—can, by their free will be anywhere they want to be in the universe. That is the way she comes to you because you want her to, and she wants to. It has to be a mutual thing. She has the ability to tap into any vibration that she wants except, as she said, your physical health and finances, as these are God things.

With her vibrational abilities, she can pluck songs out of the ether, control electrical current, create sounds like the horn honks and telephone rings, and talk with you through your mind. Any vibrational thing she can control because everything you think is solid on your plane is only vibrations put together to materialize your body, your home, your cars, et cetera. Quantum physics is only now starting to understand that.]

Tuesday Morning, April 12

[Hi. Where are you now?]
I am in the same place. I am learning valuable lessons of further love for my soul. These are being taught to me by my spirit guides and my guardian angel. Physically, I am in an area out of what you would call your space. It is in our universe, not in another dimension of earth. The universe is only one of several universes that I am now aware of. I

can be anywhere I want to be in the universe. It is impossible for you to conceive what is going on. It is a different realm.

Just know that I am all right, joyous, and surrounded by love. I wish I could explain it better in terms that you can understand. By the way, you noticed that I honked the horn last night to tell you that I am still with you and that I am all right. Also gave you the direction when you were awake that I can do many things for you.

As I mentioned, what I cannot do is to really help you with any money situation. That is the realm of God through the law of attraction and your free will. Also, your physical health is a God intervention that you can determine through your mind, using the law of attraction. An emotional, positive healthful feeling will give you great health, and a negative emotion will undermine your physical health.

Please now spend a couple of hours a day typing all of these notes until you can catch up. It is very important that you write this book. I think that you are getting over all of the enormous emotional ups and downs of my passing. Please remember that I am here with you always when you want me to be. One of the important things that I have to do is to help take care of your emotional needs because I love you so much. Our love vibrations are similar. Have a happy day.

Love,

Suz

Chapter 9

◇◆◇◆◇◆◇

CONTINUING ON WITH SIGHTINGS AND SOUNDS

Thursday Morning, April 14

[All of these happenings make me feel secure that Sue is still with me and solidify my thoughts about life after death. The books I am reading are interesting in that these happenings have not only happened to me, but they have a pattern with many other people who have lost loved ones. These patterns are very similar and not way out from each other, which validates my thinking that there is a common thread involved in the transition and life in heaven.

I do not know how long these activities will go on. I intelligently know that she is in heaven, but I am only now emotionally realizing that she is there. I no longer have to worry about her. I hope these activities will continue for as long as I am still here on earth. In one of the books I read, the author said such activities had been going on for three years as of that writing and still continued.

I asked Sue yesterday about another sign, as I really like Sue's tangible showings from time to time. Last night I woke up about 2:30, and as I was lying in bed, a little brown dog appeared for less than five seconds, lying in what appeared to be a window frame high up above the foot of the bed. Even though the bedroom was dark, the window was lighted quite brightly, so I saw the dog extremely well.

Sue had a little border collie she named Shep that she had to leave behind in Vermont when she moved here, since he had been raised and was living happily on a farm. She often wondered about the dog and was interested what had become of Shep, as it was a number of years ago. I wondered if she was showing me this dog and if it was Shep. This must have been a manifestation like the blue jay.

I was about to get up to go to the bathroom, which is around the corner from the bedroom, when in my mind I heard her say, "Don't get up yet. I am not through." Then a bright light from the bathroom came on for about three seconds and was reflected on the lower portion of the bedroom, just outside of the bathroom.

After a few minutes, I went into the bathroom and used the dimmer switch to turn the lights on low. Again, as in February, the two upper lights came on dim, just like normal, but the light that is on the same circuit, the one over the enclosed shower came on very bright and started flashing, just like the ones in the dining room had done in the nights after her passing. I then switched the lights off. I turned the lights back on, and they came on as they normally do. In the sixteen years that we have lived here, the lights have always worked perfectly.]

Friday Morning, April 15

[Thanks again for sending me a sign last night that you are all right.]

Well, you had asked for a sign again, so I thought this might be a good way to do it, like I did it last night. Things are the same with me. Nothing has changed except I am growing stronger in my spirit and in my identity here, with the help of my angels that are kind of shepherding me through the change from earth to heaven. I am in a growth period of my spirituality.

As I have mentioned, there is no time factor here. Spirit guides would like to simplify a little about some things you would like to know. Hope it is of interest.

Spirit Guides:[Yes, she is fine, and, as she says, she is in a different world now and is happy and joyful.

[Will she continue to contact me?]

Yes, if you want her to. She will only come when you want her to. She does not want to interfere with your life now.

[Where is she?]

As she told you, on a different plane, which is a little below us but not too far. It is a gradual transition from life on your planet to life on another plane, as will happen to you when you die. So enjoy yourself on your beautiful earth, and live life to the fullest.

[Where is this other plane?]

Everywhere in the cosmos—what you call the universe. Just as light passes throughout the universe, everyone that passes can travel through and around the universe if they want to. Many want to stay connected to their previous life and world, like Sue does, to be with and help their loved ones still on earth. I should have said the universe and beyond.

[What does beyond mean?]

There is more to God's universe than you on earth have found out or know. The cosmos stretches to more than infinity.

[Who created all of this?]

The Universal Spirit that you call God. You just can't begin to understand this with your—by that I mean, man's—consciousness or to see the big—and I mean, big—picture. Please do not try. Just enjoy your life.]

I am glad that you had a massage yesterday, as you seem to be more relaxed today. I know that this has been quite an ordeal and experience for you to comprehend all this, to change your thinking and completely readjust your life. It takes time, but I am always here for you. There is a tremendous amount of love between us. When you look at my pictures every once in a while, I can really feel it.

Love, your helpful wife

Please take your time typing all this up.

Saturday Morning, April 16

I am glad you did not go to the craft show today, as it will continue snowing all day. You need to spend today at home, cleaning up and going through all of the items you want to give or throw away. Also, that will give you time to reorganize your business and type more of these writings.

I see you are rereading parts of the *Everything Happens for a Reason* book. What is said on page fourteen, second paragraph, about communication with vibratory energy is correct.

As you know, our consciousness, personality, and who we are, like I am talking to you now, all remain the same. Our consciousness is not located in our physical brain. Our brain is the controller of our physical body. Everything else is pure energy. I can be anywhere I want to be, do anything I want to do, as long as it is pure love, which God is—all of that, along with the spiritual growth and soul growth to take me to an even higher level of consciousness.

It is like living on earth without having the physical body. Your scientists are in the dark ages of knowing and trying to figure out the universe. Our consciousness—who we are—never dies. Never goes away. We are in a different phase of our existence. It is as if I traveled to a different world, which I did, only one without the framework as you know it. Just impossible to explain on your earthly level; that is why you must have faith. The cloud right now is the best way to describe it. I am going to let you get along with your work, as we could talk all day long, and you would not get anything done.

I think it is nice that you want to look at my pictures every day and remember me on earth in our lives together. Short, wasn't it, but happy. As they say, time flies. Please enjoy every hour, every minute, of every day now. Life is too short to waste any of it, isn't it? Don't you hate that expression everyone uses? But it is true, isn't it?

Suz

Sunday Morning, April 17, Alarm Box Again

[Thank you for putting me in touch with the Eterena website. I also found a website called The Afterlife Advocate.]

Well, I thought that would be interesting for you, since you are examining life after death for our book. You and I will write this book, and we can have it published, even though it might be self-published. We will see where it goes. Hopefully, at least one copy will get into the hands of someone that has a lot of grief over a loved one's death. If it helps only one person, then it is worthwhile. Also, it will be a record for you of our talks, but probably it will help many people.

[Interesting that yesterday night, Saturday early morning, the alarm box sounded off with pings and the little light turned on because it is tied in with electricity, but it is not hooked up to work now.]

Yes, I thought that would be of interest to you as another sign. Fun, isn't it? You know that I am all right and active where I am. I know that there are many inches of snow on the ground, so I am going to let you go so you can clear off the car and go to church. See you in church!

Love,

Suz

Sunday Evening, April 17

My spirit guides, my guardian angel, and other angels are helping me in many ways. My soul is expanding to foster even more love and beauty. This is being done not by sitting in any formal way, like a classroom on earth; at least right now. It is learning being transmitted to me by telepathy. I am growing in my love of God. I am like floating in a beautiful cloud with beautiful music all around me. There is another level that I will go to, I am told, but I do not know the details yet.

I know it is frustrating to you not to have concrete answers, but I don't know them yet. Maybe one of your days, I can give you more information as I learn it. Some of those descriptions of the near-death experiences are invalid, although most of them are correct. Just know that I am obviously committed to communicate with you as we have been doing, since our vibrations are pretty well attuned to each other.

As your other vibrations get higher, which they will, then I believe that you will get to see me, maybe just for an instant, and I will be able to have you feel my touch, perhaps on your cheek. There are many different set of vibrations emitting from you, as from all earthly people, and like I say, those need to get higher and stronger. Our love vibrations are very high and strong, which enables us to talk through your mind to be able for you to journal. I will mention to you, which I know other people will think strange, but I have the ability to see through your eyes from time to time. I can see a beautiful day and the beautiful mountains.

We are very close together—you in your world, and me being able to talk with you at any time when you want me to and still allow me to do what I want and have to do where I am. As I have mentioned many times, people on earth can't begin to understand where we are (I am), so please take it on faith. As you know, I am with love, intense love all around me. Just enjoy our communication.

Suz

Please try to catch up on your typing of these written pages.

Monday Morning, April 18

[Hello.]

Hi. You seem to really be starting to tune in to me, like never before. I know that this has been very traumatic for you—my death/leaving earth. It has changed your thinking and your emotions for the best, your consciousness, and even, to a degree, your soul. You now have a definite belief in God, where before, like most people, [it was] nebulous. You know that there is a Higher Intelligence to all of this because of my transformation to a higher life. This will change your whole life for the better. I guess you should keep a pen and paper near your bed at night so you do not forget some of the things that come to you.

I mentioned last night in your mind that I can do all of the things I need to do to improve and engage my soul, deepen my love, get closer to God, learn all of the universal knowledge, and still be with you when you need and want me to. I know you went to the seminar on healing at the church yesterday afternoon because I was with you, even though you did not know it. It was interesting that God came to him with his talent, asked him to be a healer, and to spend the rest of his life healing people. I can tell that you feel lighter this morning, and something is working. He knows and believes that there is a life after death, and this reinforces your beliefs.

Remember that I have to talk with you using your vocabulary, which does not always allow me to give you my pure thoughts, although most of them come through. I don't know that any of this communication would be happening if we had stayed with a so-called normal church, as most people think about a church. By your finding the philosophy of our new church and all of the classes you took, it certainly opened and widened your mind to a belief in God and all that entails. You have a lot of typing to do, so I am going to let you go for now, and you can continue your workday as well. Remember that I am with you, and my love for you deepens every day. I know right now, for some odd reason, you think sometimes that you don't deserve it, but that is hooey.

Sue

Tuesday April 19th

[Will you keep giving me signs that I can put into this book?]

You know, God wants us to write this book. I will continue giving you signs, and as I progress where I am, you will receive other information that will make the book interesting. Don't worry about that.

[It seems strange to me to receive your thoughts without your being here physically.]

I know, but that is the way, obviously, that it has to be. I know that you are still a little concerned about my love, but I have no idea why. I love you deeply, or we would not be talking in this way.

Sue

Wednesday Morning, April 20, First Fragrance Scent

[Last night I awakened and immediately smelled the strong scent of a light fruity lemon fragrance, and I recognized the scent of the body wash that Sue used all of the time.]

Did you smell my fragrance last night? I thought this was the one that you would recognize. I know you are concerned about the typing and format of this book, but it is fairly simple and easy. You will work it out.

I am still in the first level of heaven. It is a growing level, kind of like when you first start kindergarten. You don't know what to expect on that first day. Everything is new and strange, but you have a teacher or teachers that will take care of you, explain things, and walk you through it. This is kind of where I am now, but there is no feeling of strangeness, just a feeling of love and peace. There is a lot of music, very beautiful, soft, and relaxing. I know who I am, I know who you are, and I really remember my life on earth.

I am like in a large room without any walls, and my friends and past relatives are with me. My teachers are angels that are so loving, tender, and kind; it is unbelievable. I have a lot to learn, and I understand that I will progress through stages of my existence now. Since I am joyful and there is no time here, I am looking forward to the next phase of my new life, but there is no hurry. It will be interesting to see what comes in the future.

Love,

Suz

Please keep your vibrations up so we can communicate on an even deeper level. I know that you would like some more tangible evidence, such as seeing me for a split second or two. It will come. Please be patient, but you have to develop a higher vibration without much sadness. I know you will get there. It takes time. It has only been a few short months now.

Thursday, April 21

[Hi. I smelled a different fragrance last night. It was your natural lovely scent."

Yes, that is right. I was there to show you again that I am fine and love you so much.

"Again, where do you fit into all of this?]

I am in our—your —universe, but on a different level. A level of—your earthly vocabulary is a problem for me now—of life. I have no physical body, of course, but I am again like a misty cloud, which does contain my personality, my spirit, my soul, who I am. There is teaching and learning to develop my soul. My personality and my spirit remain the same as they were on earth, and obviously I retain my memory of all of the things I did on earth. I am me, so don't worry about that. I have let go of all of my earthly baggage, as there is no physical body to have the physical problems that you all have.

There is no negative emotion; all positive vibrations of love and joy and happiness. I am floating in a cloud of serenity. I am not just out in space. I am in a localized area, which, if you want, you can call another dimension, but that is not a complete description. Look at it this way. You are living in a dimension of earth that basically, according to quantum physics, is a vibrational field. Everything you think is solid is just vibrations held together by electromagnetic forces. That is why I can come through to you the way I have.

The lights flickering on and off, the songs, and your phone ring, the bicycle horn, and the blue jay are types of manifestations. I know it is impossible to wrap your mind around all of that. Think of my being with everyone that has ever lived, in a place like earth but with no physical dimensions, like you think you have. Please don't try to rethink this. Your scientists are just now trying to unravel the secrets of the universe but with limited ability to do that. I know this all sounds strange to you.

Please live your life the way you have been enjoying the earthly life. We have—you now have—a beautiful planet, a beautiful world, so enjoy it while you can, and do not try to rethink it. You are on earth, like I was, to grow your spirit but primarily to grow your soul. I know all of this sounds weird to you, but live your life in the vein of the Golden Rule. You will be happier if you do that. Someday, perhaps in a long number of years, you will join me, and all will become known.

This is the best that I can do now. Maybe later I can describe what is going on and where I am in a little bit better way that you can understand.

Sue

Chapter 10

SPIRIT GUIDES, BUMBLEBEE, AND FRAGRANCES

Thursday Morning, April 21, Spirit Guides

Spirit Guides:[We are all spirit guides, and Sue said it would be all right and does not mind if we follow up with you on what she has just said about where she is. The only reason we are pursuing this line of thought is for some clarification.

We are many years older than new spirits and souls that come to heaven. Heaven is a multilevel place, where there are many levels of people, if you would rather have that word to better understand. Call it many dimensions—although that word is not right, it is something you can understand. It—heaven, if you like that word also—is a place that is close to God in His heavens. Climbing up the levels is done through the growth of the soul.

There are teachers—angels are an apt description for you; however, there are other names for the teachers also. We are sorry you, just as earthlings, cannot understand that. Jesus is God's Son, and He came to earth to teach God's Word. The best advice we can give you is the word *faith*. You must develop and have faith that there is a reason for all this. You know by now that your earth world is not a solid place. Nothing is solid, but it seems so to you, or you could not live your life there. Faith is believing someone or something when you can't prove it is real, but you have complete trust in it.]

Saturday Morning April 23

Hi. What is it you wish to know?

[I guess I want to know where you are now, as I am a little concerned since everything is a mystery to me.]

I am in heaven and have lots of flowers around me. As you know, I love flowers and have been good at arranging them all of my earthly life. They are magnificent, with colors that you do not have. The grass is green, and everything is lush here. My spirit guides that I had on earth are still with me, as they go with me wherever I go to help my transition from earthly life to death—I mean a transition in heaven from one place to another level of consciousness. This life is like the life on earth but without the physical body or any negative emotions.

I see that you are wondering about houses and buildings because you have read about that in books. I do not know yet, as I am not on that level. I am just resting in my garden of flowers now. As time goes on—your saying, as we do not have time here—I will learn a lot more. As you know, I will be between here and earth to show you my signs, like the bumblebee yesterday.

[I saw a beautifully colored large bumblebee, the first I have seen of the season, as I sat in my car in a parking lot. It flew up and landed on my driver's side mirror and just stayed in the same spot for several minutes while I was engrossed in reading a book. I rolled the window up, as I was concerned it would fly into the car. After a while, the bee flew off and went as far as I could see. A few minutes later, the bee was back and just sat in the same spot on the mirror for several minutes until I had to drive off. It is interesting that some of the books I am reading mention that people have seen butterflies and even birds in unusual circumstances after their loved ones have died.]

Please bear with me on your questions, and as I develop more learning, I will describe my future here as it unfolds.

Spirit Guides again: [You asked Sue about houses. Houses in heaven are abodes that keep the personalities of spirits separate from each other so they can haves places to go for meditation, learning, and privacy when they want to. They are made of vibrations, just like yours are on earth. People (spirits) don't just lie around on clouds all day long. Heaven is another world without the problems of earthly worlds. It is all-encompassing, and it is immense, with as many universes as you know put together, even more than that.

Just know that Sue is in a wonderful place with a wonderful life and can communicate with you whenever she wants to. She will tell you more as she develops her life. She has been here for only a little while. Please be patient, and you will know a lot more in a while.]

Sunday Afternoon, April 24, Another Fragrance

[Yesterday after church I went to a seafood restaurant for lunch, the same one where I frequently took Sue after church for lunch or dinner. I sat in the same area where we used to sit. It really gave me some comfort. I was reading one of the new books about heaven, and I had just finished eating when, all of a sudden, I smelled a very strong fragrance that got stronger with every breath. There were not any other diners around me, so I knew it was Sue. I was kind of shocked and asked the waiter if he smelled anything and where it was coming from. He sniffed around but said he could not smell anything—he probably thought I was daft.

I think Sue just wanted to give me a sign that she knew I was at the restaurant and that she was pleased. It amazed me that the waiter could not smell anything, as it was very strong. Perhaps in this case it was just meant for me, and for some reason she did not want anyone else to smell the very strong fragrance.]

Monday Night, April 25

I tried to come to you last night because I know you would like a concrete vision of me, even for a split second or two. However, I cannot lower my vibrations any lower, and your vibrations are not high enough yet. In due time, I think this will work, as you are starting in the morning to meditate, as one of the books suggested.

[I had a strong dream last night where I dreamed that I saw in the hospital Sue's spirit leave her earthly body and soar up out of it. It was quite real for a dream, but it was only a dream.]

I know your dream last night, and that was kind of what happened after my death. I have described that light at the end of the tunnel. I think that, subconsciously, most earth people believe that there is a heaven, but their egos will not let them rethink that because it is too dangerous to the ego, as the ego does not last after death. The ego is there to protect you on earth, especially at a young age. Some people think that as an adult, the ego is no longer necessary for protection, but the ego will not let go.

[Tell me again how you do signs. I have read that matter is crystallized energy.]

By the use of electromagnetic energy. We are all energy even though we (you) appear solid. So by using the energy of the universe through the use of your electric current, I can manipulate the energy in any electrical or electronic device. Thus, the ceiling lights, the alarm switch, the computer and radio waves are very easy.

The same with your cell phone; the songs I selected were meant to be messages to you. Unfortunately, the songs that I wanted to send you with the messages that I would like to have sent were not written or sung yet, so I do not have access to them. How I do this is so strange to you that it is just not possible to explain it to you. So please just know that it is easy for me or anyone else that has departed, if they want to. I know that in the books you are reading now that this is not exclusive to me. It has happened to many people that are left behind when their loved one departs.

I will continue to give you signs of my well-being but probably not as dramatic as in the past, as I know that you know that I continue to live and be myself in a happy, joyful, loving, and being-loved way. So long for now.

Love,

Your wife,

Sue

Wednesday Morning, April 27

Good morning. I feel that you have gotten over your grief and sorrow because you know that I am alive and joyful in my world, with unconditional love for you and everyone that I come in contact with. It has been a long and painful ride for you since my death, even though the sorrow has been slowly going away. It has still taken a long time. What if there was no life after death? Then the grief and pain would probably last the rest of your life.

See how people feel that do not have the knowledge that you now have. This is why we are writing this book. Thank you for picking my beautiful tulips and putting them in a vase next to my pictures. That was very thoughtful of you. I know you did this even though we had not discussed it. Continue on today.

Love, regards,

Suz

[Hi. How can you talk through my mind?]

We can do anything on earth for you, as long as it is within God's frame of love.

[What about other inhabitable planets? Are there any? And, of course, we have legs and arms to move about, lungs to breath, eyes and ears to hear and see, a body that carries our brains and mind.]

They have their own identities, features, and life-forms. We don't go there because we are not like them. They have their own version of heaven, where they go when they transition. There are many universes, not just ours. God put together a plan for life of many kinds. Those different lives are based on their planets' own structures. We call them aliens for lack of a better word. In essence, they are alien to earth's world. However, they are certainly equal to us in God's eyes.

[I know you don't know any more details on this at your level.]

Saturday Morning, April 30

[Hi. How are you now? I understand that you just think and manifest what you want.]

I am fine. I am sitting in my garden on the park bench. The flowers are boundless. The trees are beautiful. The colors are much more vivid than on earth. There are mountains in the distance and a beautiful blue sky above. I know it sounds like earth, and, in a sense, it is.

[I heard a remark, stated many years ago, by someone who said, 'Thus we will come to know, within ourselves, that there is no death and that only a veil divides, as thin as gossamer.' I thought that was interesting.]

We are not very far from you but a completely different cycle of vibration. Without a body, we do not need any food or water. Our spirit just lives, and we think, act, and live, just like you but in a glorious environment of God's heaven.

[Last night I heard your soft voice as I was awakening, and you said you were there. On the bedroom ceiling, I saw some small sparkling stars every once in a while—not many but definitely small sparkling stars in a completely black room.]

Yes, I am still trying to show you myself, but I am still having a hard time lowering my vibrations enough. I will be able to do it sometime in the future. As we go on, maybe this will all start making sense to you as I progress in my new journey.

Sunday Morning, May 1

[I was home, feeling very sick with bronchitis and a cold, and I went to lie down in bed about 2:30 in the afternoon. Just after I got into bed, I heard a loud horn honk from Sue's bedside, just once. I realized that she was reminding me that she was all right. I think she is doing this to give me comfort, since I am still grieving a little because she is not physically with me, even though I know she is alive in heaven. It immediately cheered me up, and I took a nap.]

Sunday Afternoon, May 1

Hi. What do you want to talk about?

[Whatever you want.]

You are reading some more of the books about life-after-death communications. I can feel that your consciousness is rapidly still changing to realize there is a whole new life after death. It takes time to think about it and dwell on it, even after you have had all these somewhat dramatic signs. All of your life you have thought about death as being permanent, like everyone else. It is all so brand new to you, this concept of another world, that even with our talks it is only gradually dawning on you.

What your new book says—that we should live a life of love and compassion and not just run after the material things that will not go with us—is certainly true. Even though you felt sick today, I am glad you could stay home and rest for the first time in about the three months that I have been gone from your life on earth. It is important to get my story out there with the others. Each ADE incident is a little different in the results of how the loved ones are contacted.

I am now in the higher dimension of the first level. I am still resting before I really get into learning to increase my soul's awareness of God. I am aware of God, or I would not be on this level. My angels and spirit guides surround me and are letting me rest my spirit after such a dramatic shift from earth to heaven. I mentioned my surroundings are like a lush garden with flowers, plants, meadows, streams, shining sun, sparkling light, trees, verdant colors—like nothing on earth. All souls are in their own quietness here. All is peace. My father, my grandparents, and my friends are all able to visit me whenever I think of them to join me.

All of the bad people, the murderers, are all on the bottom dimension of this level, although when they repent, see their follies, they can move up with the help of angels. No one is really lost.

Suz

Tuesday Morning, May 3

[Vibrations interest me.]

My vibrations are so high—I mean, the vibrations of heaven are so high—that I—we—have a very difficult time coming down to earth's low vibrations.

That is why you read in the books about departeds returning to visit their earthly loved ones but can stay only for fractions of a second or just a little longer. If I had my way, I would come down and join you for dinner to talk in person for a while, but then I would belong to earth again, wouldn't I? Would I then have the joy, the delightful, unforgiving love, and feel the fullness of God but have my imperfect body? I think not. If the vibrations of heaven would equal the vibrations of earth, with all of your negative emotions—harm sometimes to others, fear, jealously, envy—then it wouldn't be heaven, so what, then, would be the point of God's heaven? Does any of this make sense to you?

I am in a completely different world, an area that is as large as all of the universes put together, and there are many—many. There is no geographical limitation for me. I can be anywhere I want to be and still have a base from which to reside. I am watched over and loved and taught by my guardian angel, other angels, and my spirit guides, which are always with me as they were on earth. They don't come to me or interfere with me unless I call on them for help or answers.

As we proceed, I will learn more about all of the levels and what they mean and be able to discuss this with you.

So long for now.

Love,

Suz

Wednesday Morning, May 4

[Sue, boy, you are sure taking care of me. It is 8:45 in the morning, and I thought that I would get a massage. I tried to call for an appointment three times, but my telephone would not even ring. I heard some intermittent tones instead of ringing. I then called my office to see if the phone would ring. It did, and I found out that my real estate floor shift was starting at 11:15 instead of instead of 2:30, like I thought. My phone would not ring the health parlor but would ring my office.]

Yes, I knew that you had made a mistake so I wanted you to realize that, as there is a hundred-dollar fine if you missed your floor appointment. I started to come to you last night but you were having bad dreams so I stayed away; maybe tonight. I am glad you are accumulating these books on after-death communications. This last one is very scientific from this doctor and is very illuminating (pun) to you. I am glad that you have the desire to look into this as much as possible to try to understand not only what is going on but how and why. Although you now have read so many accounts from so many sources, you are really getting a feel for what happens after we die.

It is too bad that even when most people read what you are writing and will read about what is happening in my new life, most will not believe. Hopefully, it will start some people thinking about that.

Suz

Friday Morning, May 6

[What do you do?]

I am learning, being taught by my teachers. My teachings are about expanding my consciousness of love, God, increased intelligence, beauty, and even fun where I am. There is a wealth of information—all of the wisdom that has ever been thought by earthly people and music by the masters. I can hear any music I want—operas and popular songs. I can even sing with my friends. It is like I am in a great park of physical beauty. I look like I did when I was fifty years old. From my pictures you know how pretty and mature I was at fifty. My body is complete, although I usually wear a whole flowing gown, very sparkling.

I have not been here long enough to be at the level of houses, museums, schools, where I can just relax and enjoy the almost physical presence of structures like I just mentioned. I am going to keep sending you signs, the reason being that it is so strange coming from where your beliefs were that I want you to know that I am alive and happy so you

Chapter 11

FIRST FACIAL SIGHTING/ CONTINUING MESSAGES

Friday Mid-Morning, May 6, Facial Appearance

[I was sitting in my office this morning and told Sue that I would really like to see her whenever possible. I had my eyes closed and was concentrating on a meditation that seemed to lower my brain waves from beta down to alpha.

All of a sudden, with my eyes closed, something happened that has never happened before. I felt shivers and goose bumps. I saw, in my mind's eye, a circle of very intense black. It was a blast of black, like a fireworks display in a dark sky. As I concentrated on it, a dark blue and violet light started to swirl around and shift the colors, like a violet-blue cloud mist.

A face was trying to develop from the dark blue color swirl. I finally saw a large beautiful eye and eyebrow appear, kind of like you would see in a cosmetic advertisement. The eyebrow and eye were greatly oversized. They were beautiful, all blue and violet color, with the eye and eyebrow appearing in the blue color. Then the right eye appeared as the left-eye picture disappeared. I did not see a full face, just a partial face with beautiful eyes and eyebrows and a little face area under the eye. It was all in vivid hues of dark blue, medium blue, and dark violet, all swirling around. It lasted a full three or four minutes, with the facial features appearing and then disappearing and reappearing. This happened again and again.

After a while, it started to disappear and then completely disappeared. I think that I was so shocked that I started to come out of the meditation, and that may have made it disappear.]

"Sue, what happened? I am still stunned."

You said you wanted to see me, and so it was time. I managed to force my vibrations to your level and, with your lowered brain waves, show you as much of my face as I could. Now that you have stopped grieving and are really not as sad, I am not being held back by your grief and sorrow. Instead of seeing something out in the room, since it was full daylight, this was the best way.

Monday Morning, May 9

I am learning about the seven levels of heaven, although I am now solidly in the third level of heaven, thanks to you for getting over your grief that holds us all back. I want to stay even closer than I am now to try to help you continue to get over your tremendous grief. Sadness is okay for you, and you will probably have a certain amount of sadness for me throughout the rest of your life. This is human and does not affect me.

I have friends that I knew on earth, and I am making friends with other spirits that I like. It is like coming back home to be closer to God, who is on the seventh level with all of the angels and masters. The masters are spirits and souls that have worked their way through all of the levels, having attained complete, loving consciousness. Everything is love and various degrees of love, which is hard to explain to you from our individual vantage points.

I am going to continue giving you signs of my well-being so that you will not digress from your continued healing. Death is such a shock to those left behind that we need to help you overcome it. Right now, I can't explain the complexities of all life on earth and the reason for it, other than it is a growth period for the soul. Just have faith that everything turns out all right and the way God wants it to.

Note:[Faith is defined as belief with strong conviction; belief in something for which there may be no tangible proof; complete trust; confidence; release or devotion. Faith is the opposite of doubt.]

Ward, I now know that you also believe in God through my death and my renewal of life in heaven. Without God there would not be a loving world, where I am, and death would be death. Jesus rose, and other religions, East and West, believe in God, although with other names.

Must be something to this, right? Have faith.

Suz

[As I drove out yesterday from a fast-food restaurant drive-through window, another lone bumblebee flew in front of my windshield and stayed there, looking at me, for a few seconds until I turned into the street. This is now the third sighting of a lone bumble bee in the last ten days.]

[Last night I was awakened by a pop-like sound emanating from the bedroom TV, which was turned off. Right after that, I smelled Sue's strong fragrance of the lemon fruit-flavored body wash. It was in the room for about thirty seconds.]

Thursday Morning, May 12

I am on the third level of heaven now, and I am learning all about the complex aspects of heaven. There are many universes, of which ours (yours) was just one—and a small one at that. God created the whole cosmos and everything in it. God is the name we use for the All Intensive Creator that created out of love—a Mighty Invisible Force that I am only starting to learn about. It was an intense desire of a Super Being to want to expand his love throughout infinity, at that time the void of space.

It is incomprehensible to explain this loving, immense power source we call God. I am only now getting a glimpse into what makes up the total picture of the dynamic, unfolding creation. I will discuss more on this later as I learn and will try to explain the inexplicable. We will see what I come up with as I gain greater knowledge from my teachers. The dense vibrations of earth are the lowest in all of the known universes, as far as I can tell.

That is why it is so difficult for any of us to come to you and stay very long. It takes up too much energy. You read all about the after-death communication in your books, and none of the situations that involve after-death communication are for very long at a time. Most people don't realize that there is life after death and don't even try to communicate with their deceased loved ones. Only for the protection of their loved ones will they come forth with a message, even though they watch over them all of the time.

Friday Morning, May 13

[This is remarkable, seeing almost your whole face, which I am trying to see now through meditation.]

Yes, I am showing you my face, as that is something you recognize and can understand. As you know, I really don't have a body unless I project one. In heaven I can project all of the time, especially the body that I am used to, the body I had on earth. Toward the end today, you saw a kind of a whole circle in the middle of the blackness. That is my whole spirit. The deeper you go into the alpha phase, the more you can pick up my features. Your brain in alpha, as opposed to beta, lets my consciousness come through your mind. The words here are immaterial, as it really does not describe fully describe the process.

Basically, it is my vibrations coming down, and your vibration in alpha coming up that makes the connection possible. As you know, with your eyes closed when you see the really deep, swirling shades of violet, dark blue, and black, you know that we are connected. Then, as I mentioned, I show you the features of my face, as that is what you understand. My features are oversized, like large eyes and eyebrows, much bigger than you would see if I were there in person. That is just the way I come through. The one instance that you saw a full face was rare, but maybe we can work together to have me bring more of a full face.

I think it is more fun and gives you more pleasure to see me instead of just talking through your mind. It just gives you more emotional satisfaction; I can tell.

Sunday Morning, May 15

God is in seventh heaven, the seventh level, although His essence is everywhere on all levels, all universes, as well as on earth. Then when you say on earth—the term you use when something is perfect—"I am in seventh heaven," it must be in inscribed in people's consciousness. From where it comes, I don't know, but it must be a universal thought, perhaps in subconscious knowledge of God and heaven.

The third level of heaven is the beginning of our souls' learning of the complexities of God. It is developing more of our ability to love and be of service wherever we are needed. Advanced souls, like spirit guides, help those less advanced enlarge the fullness of their beings. It is very mysterious to you and hard for me to explain to you.

People on earth, with all of the infirmities and problems, as well as all of the wonderful happenings, have a need for help many times in their lives. Everyone has spirit guides; their sole purpose is to render advice and sometimes aid when and where needed, when asked. The reason many people are not helped is because they don't realize that they have spirit guides available to them.

Angels are above spirit guides in complexity and enlightenment. Angels are more powerful than spirit guides and are available to watch over you and are able to physically intervene in times of trouble, if they feel that they are wanted. Because you have free will, they cannot and will not interfere with that.

Monday Morning, May 16

I am glad that you bought our minister's CDs of his sermons of last year on life after death. You didn't realize how much he believed in life after death. My consciousness is developing from my teachers, spirit guides, angels, and master souls. We call them master teachers. The point is to increase our consciousness level higher and higher. For example, your abilities are on a certain earthly level and only grow as generations go by. You, in 2016, have developed a much greater consciousness than generations ago, and they were more developed than the caveman. On my level, we can learn and don't have to wait for a generational advance.

As we develop, then we are able to see what the next level of heaven is all about, and with that knowledge we can progress there, on and on to the very highest level, and obtain angel status. There are billions of angels. It is a journey to have me grow so that in the future I can become one of them and help new people as they come through. It is an ongoing process, just like life on earth is an ongoing process. As our consciousness increases, then we move up the ladder of heaven's levels. As an analogy, a kindergartener cannot be a college student without physical and mental growth along the way.

First, we gain spirit guide status. It is a wondrous thing, which unfortunately leaves all on your planet in the dark about that, so you must enjoy your life now, day to day, minute to minute, and let evolution follow. Again, have faith that what happens after your life is over is what is happening to me, and it is. As you know, heaven is heaven, with all of the wondrous happenings. Good-bye for now.

Suz

Tuesday Morning, May 17

[I am just starting to believe, as opposed to intelligently know, that you are in heaven, in joy, and showered in love.]

Yes, all of that is true, but as you have been reading, light is the most powerful, blessed part of all. God is light. I saw—and other people that passed at the time saw—a powerful bright light, shining at the end of the tunnel leading out from earth into heaven. You can't imagine the love shining in and from that light.

[I have not had a sign in the last few days.]

You really have not asked for one, and because you have been sick with that bronchitis, I have not intervened. Now that you are well, we shall see. The reason for signs from me is to let you know that I am fine and alive in heaven. You know that now, however, it is nice for you to feel closer to me with some kind of physical sign from me, either my presence, lights, some kind of noise, or even seeing me, as I learn more how to come through to you. The easiest thing for me is my fragrance, which you have noticed a little the last two nights.

Wednesday Morning, May 18

[Last night I awakened at 4:15 and went to the bathroom. On my way, I thought that I hadn't had a sign from Sue for a couple of days, other than her fragrance. I was thinking that it made me comfortable to have a sign once in a while. We are journaling always, but actually having a sign sometimes was wonderful. I went back to bed. Our bedroom is always black without the lights on. After I was in bed for five or six minutes, the bottom of the bedroom wall outside of the bathroom was illuminated by a light coming from the bathroom. The light then burned brighter for a couple of seconds, and then went out. There is not any way an outside light can come into the bathroom, as we have heavy curtains on the window, and the patio wall outside is quite high. Sue gave me the sign I asked for just a very few minutes before.]

[Thank you for the sign.]
You are very welcome. I wanted you to have a sign, not only [because] you asked and I was able to comply, but it gives me great pleasure to make you feel wanted by me. It has only been about three and a half months since my passing, and I want you to be aware that I am still here and to keep your spirits up.
Suz

Thursday Morning, May 19

[I know we talk all of the time, but I would like to do this for the book. That first day that I saw you in my mind during the meditation, I saw more of your body and much brighter than today.]

95

Yes, you were deeper in meditation than you have been lately. If you can relax and not try to see me, it may work better for you.

[Tell me more about your situation.]

I am in heaven on the third level. I was on a much lower level when I arrived, and as I have mentioned, it is a resting place for a while so we can figure out what is going on. Really realizing that death is not permanent comes as a big shock to us, and it takes a little time to acclimatize to this transition. I rested for a while and then was ready to move on with the help of my guides. Now I am really enjoying my situation and am playing with my garden while I am being taught to develop my consciousness to an even higher level.

Everything here is done by thought. When we want something, we think a thought about it, and it materializes. For example, when I want to give you a sign, I think; I give a thought to what I want, and then it appears. Remember: "As a man thinks, so he is." Another is "You become what you think about." On earth as it is in heaven, thought works the same way. If you want to change your life on earth, just change your thought to what you want. It is not rocket science. It is so simple, but you make it so hard. Relax and think of what you want, and it will happen. If it is in your best interests and in the best interests of everyone else, it will happen.

For example, you have had the experience in the past of when you want or need a cash deal in real estate, it will happen. A couple of years ago you had the thought that you wanted the two closings coming up to close on your birthday, and they both closed on your birthday. It is the law of attraction in operation, combined with your thought pattern.

Saturday Morning, May 21

[Yesterday I went to get the mail out of our outdoor mailbox, and another large bumblebee swirled around my head and then flew away. There are not any other bees in the area. I love you and miss you being here with me like we were.]

I know, but it was the best thing, and you know it. You will get more energy as you keep getting well. It was bound to happen, after the few

96

hard months, that your body would react with all of the tension and make you stop and take it easy. I want you to miss me a little. If you didn't, then there wouldn't be any love.

Sue

Monday Morning, May 23

[I went to a different church yesterday to hear and see a minister who is well recognized. He's from out of the country and was talking about how many people are leaving the formal organized religious church due to the fact that they see God in a different light than the approach for centuries that talks about a sometimes vengeful God. He feels that organized religion during the earlier Christian Church got away from a loving God for their own ends of keeping the flock in control.

He said the Bible, especially the Old Testament, was rewritten many times over the centuries for the benefit of kings or a church that wanted their particular views promoted. Some of the Dead Sea scrolls and other documents now turning up suggest that scenario. He said we need to get back to the God that is in our hearts, that Christianity is now looking for new beginnings. It is a very interesting scenario.]

I am glad that you went to see him, as it will help you continue your search for your expanded consciousness while living on earth.

Spirit guides again:

Spirit Guides:[Continue on your path to develop your compassion for other people, animals, and all life. You can also show and develop compassion, believe it or not, for your earth, flowers, trees, and all of God's living things. As you know, you have had mostly self-interest, except for Sue, most of your life, as has everyone else, so that in itself is not a bad thing, as it does promote other people's needs and desires, although inadvertently.

You are a good man (person) with few exceptions, and not only have you forgiven yourself, but God has forgiven you also, as you now know right from wrong. Continue on with your life.]

Tuesday Morning, May 24

[I heard a loud ringing sound from your little box of clothes that I have kept in the bedroom with some things in it for sentimental sake about 1:30 last night, but nothing else happened. I did smell your fragrance so strongly; it was very sensitive to my nostrils.]

Yes, I wanted you awake, as I was trying to materialize like you want me to, but it still is hard for me to get down to your earth vibration level. Maybe someday that will happen as I grow larger in spirit where I am. So don't be discouraged, as I can show you other signs as your time goes on.

Thursday Morning, May 26

[Hi. Anything new for you?]

Yes, I am learning from my teachers more about the universe and God. Actually, I am sitting, believe it or not, in a beautiful classroom with other people, just like school on earth, just that this room has no walls, just stools and chairs. There is no need for walls as we don't have any weather here. All is light, like sunshine on earth, but it is a glorious light from God. At some point in time, my decision is to help educate other people to our world as they arrive from earth after passing. As you know, I have always liked helping other people through their time of challenge, be it health or emotional problems.

I know this sounds strange but we do not just sit around on clouds for eternity. This is a working world, but it really is heaven, with all of the connotations that you have thought about. Your time on earth is also a learning experience, just as mine is here but without any negatives or health problems. The soul is very completed from your perspective, also mine, but we learn to examine the depths of our individual souls. Look up *soul's* definition in the dictionary to understand what I am talking about. I am going now. Talk to you tomorrow.

Suz

[Note: Soul: the principal of life, feeling, thought, and action in humans,

regarded as a distinct entity separate from the body and commonly held to be separate in existence from the body; the spiritual part of humans as distinct from the physical part.]

Friday Morning, May 27

[What's going on?]

Ask me a question. What would you like to know?

[What is your day like?]

Well, as you probably know, there is no day or night. Our spirits can form a body and usually do, as we are used to a body on earth, and it makes it more convenient for intermingling in our learning classes with our teachers. Our teachers have been educated by their peers to pass on their education. We can choose an area that we want to work in, just like earth. Some are educating themselves in the various sciences and are learning about the further mysteries of the universe, which are many. These new ideas and discoveries can then be passed on to your earth scientists to help them in their studies.

Remember it is said that your great scientists—like Einstein, Bell, and Edison—and educators would (and still do, I suppose) go into meditation to find answers to their questions and problems. Where do you suppose those answers came from? They came from our people here that are able to get through to them, just like I am talking to you through your mind. Fascinating, isn't it? Anyone on earth that meditates or sits quietly and waits for answers will get them in all of the various educations.

This is completely different than praying. Prayers are answered by God, sometimes with a voice in mind, or most of the time prayers are answered by things that people are praying for just happening, if the prayers are supposed to be answered. God and Jesus can also come through the meditation. It just depends on what the person is asking for—ideas for a problem, help from God, it is all available to you if one asks and allows. Hope that helps.

[Do you have classrooms?]

Yes, it is a question of having a place to go, just as on earth, for a specific lesson of our vocation we have chosen. I now have a little house that I can go to for solitude and study, and I sit in my beautiful garden that I have created. I know it is difficult to understand, but just have faith that it is a completely different world.

Suz

Suzette Delashmet Shockley at fifty-six years of age

Suzette at her wedding - December 7th, 1985

Suzette at her honeymoon in Hawaii

At the Marble, CO mill site on the National Historic Register

Colorado Great Sand Dunes, National Park

Breakfast during one of Sue's trips to Santa Fe

Sue on vacation in Winer Park, CO

Her dream car a Jaguar sedan

Chapter 12

A WORD ABOUT SUE

Suzette D. Shockley was born November 11, 1946, in Philadelphia, Pennsylvania, at the Woman's Hospital of Philadelphia and passed from this earthly life in Aurora, Colorado, at the Medical Center of Aurora Hospital. From hospital to hospital in sixty-nine years. She was a very attractive person, a loving person, and was always there to help anyone who needed it. As I mentioned in the introduction, she valued cosmetics all of her life, and by really taking care of herself, she always looked about twenty years younger than her actual age.

During those sixty-nine years she had a wonderful life and was a very lovely and loving woman. In her preteen years, in her first beauty pageant she was voted queen of the Maple Gardens, Pennsylvania, Summer Parade and had several attendants. She was a straight-A student during all of her school years and received the highest grade ever given in her high school in biology. After graduation she went on to employment as an assistant to the head of research for the University of Pennsylvania Hospital Medical Center.

After several years there, she was called to Vermont. She finished her formal schooling and became involved with a regional health organization, where she was charged with developing their state and federal grant procedures. She was very successful in doing that work.

At the same time, with her varied interests, she lived on a farm outside of Putney, Vermont, and raised sheep for their wool. She bought the very best sheep, sheared them, and had the wool dyed and made into yarn for sweaters, rugs, and other sundry items that she designed, which were sold throughout Vermont. The wool yarn became the finest available anywhere and was featured on Boston television. She had named her company Shepherds Mountain Farm.

After several years in Vermont, the country beckoned her. She and a girlfriend piled everything into her Volkswagen and traveled the United States, ending up in Denver. In Denver, to get started, she took several jobs from time to time and ended up as one of the primary recruiters for a large local college. After that, she developed a very sizeable real estate and mortgage business. Always keeping her hand in many things, she developed a large cosmetics sales business and gave talks to groups on how to redefine one's personal image.

In July 1983, she met her husband-to-be, Ward Barcafer Jr. who was also a highly successful real estate salesman. They were married on Pearl Harbor day, December 7, 1985. It is interesting that Sue's birthday was Veteran's Day, November 11.

Her interests in design were unlimited, so with her husband-to-be, she started a regional jewelry business, manufacturing and selling vintage costume jewelry made from molds she found that were designed in the 1880s. She designed and hand-painted the jewelry, had the basic pieces plated back East, and then manufactured her jewelry with her company, selling it to gift and apparel stores across the Midwest. Her design talent was such that she developed a pearlized paint and blended it with other colors to resemble the colors used at the beginning of the twentieth century. Her designs were many, with an abundance of floral designs, cherubs, moon and stars, and other fanciful items like those that were made years ago. This company was called Delashmet Design.

Unfortunately, after a few years she became ill and allergic to her painting design work and could not find anyone that could duplicate her skills. She then decided to help herself with her health and then also embarked on a career of helping people through all types of energy healing. Unfortunately, soon afterward she was brought down with a brain tumor that genetically ran in her family.

During her married years she loved to travel, so after her scuba-diving honeymoon in Hawaii, she traveled around the country with her husband as often as they could get away. She loved the wine country in California, San Francisco, Disneyland, skiing at Colorado's Winter Park resort during Christmas, Rocky Mountain National Park, Estes Park, Mesa Verde National Park, the area around Durango Colorado, Cape Cod, and the East Coast.

Probably her favorite area was Santa Fe, New Mexico, to which she made many trips to collect Southwest designs of pottery and jewelry and to visit old Pueblo ruins. This area really intrigued her because of all the many ancient cultures that lived there.

She was fairly conservative in her choice of automobiles, but all of her life she had a dream of owning a nice Jaguar sedan, so toward the later part of her life, while she was still well, she was able to buy a lovely Jaguar Vanden Plas four-door sedan, which she pampered and enjoyed for several years. It was her ultimate in cars.

Her last few months were spent fighting the effects of the brain tumor, although it was benign. Unfortunately, it was not discovered until it was too late for radiation; hence, the brain operation. Her neurosurgeon said she was a fighter and thought that not only would she survive the operation but that she would perhaps bounce back to become her normal self, even though the risks of the operation around the nerves were problematic. There was no question that it was a very risky operation, but there was no choice if she was going to regain her health and not go further downhill.

On July 24, 2015, after an eight-and-one-half-hour operation, she was received into the hospital ICU. Sometime during the first night in the ICU, the nurses felt they had to enter a breathing tube into her mouth, but in doing so, they broke off three of her beautiful veneers on the top teeth and also knocked out two of her dental implants on the bottom of her teeth. They did not save the teeth or implants, which made a concern about the need to do that. It was another thing that added to Sue's emotional situation.

Due to nerve damage, she could not swallow on the left side of her throat and had to have another operation to insert a feeding tube into her stomach. She was then fed a liquid mixture, as well as her medicine, through the tube four times a day. She could not swallow water so she could only have ice cubes for moisture, other than the liquid food.

After several days in the ICU she was transferred to a regular hospital room. All of this time, I visited her at least three times a day. One day on my way back to the hospital, I received a call from her on my cell phone. In a pathetic little voice she asked me to please come get her and take her home so she could get some food, take a bath, and take a nap. Of course, under the circumstances that was impossible. It broke my heart to hear that phone call, and I still get misty-eyed just thinking about it, although I know that she is alive and joyful in another world.

The left side of her face had nerve damage; her cheek and lip as well as her left eyelid would not close and also not let her blink. To protect the cornea, she had to wear a patch over that eye and could only see out of her right eye. She was so weak that a nurse said her body was like a rag doll. As I mentioned, she was a fighter, and her spirits were still high.

After a few days she was transferred by ambulance to a rehabilitation hospital. There, she started rehabilitation of speech therapy for her throat, occupational therapy, and, as she was in a wheelchair, physical therapy. They placed a light weight on her eyelid so her eye would close at will, although she could not read or see other than a little light and could not blink. Unfortunately, the weight came off over a period when I was not there, and the weekend nurse could not seem to place it on where it would stay. Unfortunately, that dryness caused a small hole in her cornea that we had to contend with as long as she was in this hospital. So back on went the eye patch.

After a month I brought her home, as she had made some headway in all areas. Then I was able to take her to a cornea doctor to start eliminating the cornea problem with a contact that would keep the moisture in her eye. At the same time, she had another operation to insert a small light gold weight in her upper eyelid to enable it to close. Even then she had to be taken to the doctor every week to remove and replace the protective contact lens.

Before bringing her home, I purchased a power hospital bed, a power lounge chair, and a TV for the bedroom so she could watch her favorite cooking shows. I also had a handyman install a wheelchair ramp and hand bars for the shower and the toilet. I had learned how to feed her through her tube, so that was not a problem. At night, so she would not need to get up and into the wheelchair, we used a bedpan. She used the bicycle horn to rouse me to help her two or three times a night.

I hired home care nurses to come in several hours a day to watch over her when I had to go to work or to the store for her medicine. At home she had three types of therapy, which was a little draining on her emotions and energy. Some of the health care aides were good, and some of them were bad. On the very first day, the certified home health care worker did not quite know how to handle a wheelchair. She knocked Sue out of the chair and onto the carpeted floor. Fortunately, she only wound up with an abrasion on her knee, but I had to treat that daily for about a month.

Some of them did not know how to transfer her from a wheelchair to the passenger car seat, and she slipped down onto the driveway. So I had to do their job. Some of them were good, though, so I guess it is the luck of the draw. I needed them to put an eye drop in her eye every hour, so they had to do that also when I was away. One of them, instead of keeping Sue company, was in the other room, reading her Bible when I returned from the pharmacy. I guess she had been doing that for a couple of hours. We got by, but I could see how frustrated and sad Sue was becoming.

Every day seemed to be a problem for her, and she said she wondered if she would ever get her old life back. Due to her condition, she had no privacy in her personal needs, which also upset her. She was concerned and wondered what would happen to her if something happened to me.

As mentioned, the night of the first of February was to be her last night on this earth. She passed away the next day in the hospital from the blood clots in her heart. Now that we know there is life after death, I think that the time had come when God wanted to take her to be with Him and alleviate her suffering.

A word about after her passing: this happened so quickly and at a young age, considering the average length of life now. Neither one of us had made any plans for when one of us would die. So I was faced immediately with the decision of what to do with her remains, as the first manifestations had not started, and I thought that death was final.

After talking with her relatives back East and because her father had been cremated, we thought that would be the best route to follow.

I did not know where to begin, but the hospital chaplain was very helpful and gave me the names of a couple of crematoriums that were reasonable in price and reliable. One had contracts with several mortuaries, and the prices were about half of what they would have been to go to a regular mortuary out of the Yellow Pages. Obviously, this was new to me, and I was in a tremendous amount of grief. I was well taken care of, and they explained how and what would happen.

Again, not knowing what the future was going to be after her passing and thinking that death was final, I purchased a silver item that they could put her fingerprint on, and they provided me with a couple of keepsake locks of her hair. Even though she is alive in heaven, I am glad that I have these tokens of her in this life. The cremation company sent her ashes back East to be placed in the family gravesite, so I did not have another worry from that standpoint.

This is a brief story of her life. I just wanted to give you a little insight into who she was on earth to let you have a feel of her personality that is coming through to me from her new life in heaven. We cannot in any way fully describe the wonderful fullness of the life of another human being. That remains in our hearts forever.

Chapter 13

FURTHER HAPPENINGS AND SOME INSIGHTS INTO HEAVEN

Monday Afternoon, May 27

[I was on a computer in my office and ready to sign a book contract with a publishing house that I had talked with by telephone a couple of times. All of a sudden, loudly in my mind I heard Sue. "I want you to use Hay House. I want you to use Hay House, Hay House, Hay House."

I had just about committed to another company, but her words were so very strong it made me stop and think that I had to make this change, even though it was a little embarrassing for me to back off from the other company. After all, this is actually Sue's book, and I felt strongly that this is what I should do.

Over the years Sue had purchased several books published by Hay House and their self-publishing subsidiary Balboa Press, which is known for publishing spiritual books, among others. Sue felt that they were on the front lines of publishing, with authors like Dr. Wayne Dyer, Suze Orman, Esther Hicks, Marianne Williamson, Carolyn Myss, and Christiane Northrup, among hundreds of other authors.

This made Sue feel that they would understand a book that was way out of the scheme of writing from a normal perspective.]

Monday Morning, May 30

[What is going on? Anything?]

Yes, as I mentioned, I am on the third level of the seven levels of heaven. My soul has developed quite fast in regard to my developing more unconditional love. As we know, God and His vibrations are pure love. That is what it is all about. So with that all-consuming love, in addition I am learning and developing what my specialty is going to be in heaven. With that I will be able to help anyone on earth, since earth is a training ground for the soul and character. After a while, I will be able to contribute to helping people with their vibrations that have caused their illnesses. Many people are not yet called to heaven to die because their learning work on earth is not yet completed. Yet they have either unhappiness or illness in their lives, so I am obviously not an angel or even a spirit guide, but it does not matter. I can still help if people want; that is the key. There are many, many of us that can intervene when needed. How many times have you found something that you lost or misplaced and found it by accident where you had left it. Well, that is where my vibration can come into focus and give instruction to their minds where to look. I am not there yet but hope to be in the not far distant future.

Love,

Suz

Angels will intervene when people are in what they feel is deep trouble and ask for help. Minor matters are where we can come in and give service when we know people would like and ask for help. Again, how many times have you mislaid something and prayed even a little prayer to find it. There is no need for an angel's intervention in that case. I guess you could figure that we are like angels' helpers, all through vibrations. There is a hierarchy, even in heaven, from one level to another but all in loving companionship.

Tuesday Morning, May 31

[Last night I awakened at midnight and was fully awake, lying in bed, on the right side of the bed. From the head of the bed to the far wall I saw a woman's figure walking the length in about two seconds and then disappeared. Her back was to me. She was wearing a white

115

sweater and a skirt. The sweater appeared to be like an Irish knit, and I did not see a face, just the back of her head. It was fast. The room was dark, but the figure was very easily seen. Right afterward, I had the strong scent of your favorite fragrance. After a few minutes the fragrance dissipated, and then I went back to sleep.]

Yes, that was me. I am finally able to lower my vibrations to where I can resemble an earth body. I still cannot refine my facial features, so that is why I need for you to see the back of my figure. I think this all came about because you have practically eliminated all of the grief that you have felt. Now you will probably have some sorrow that I am not anymore with you, especially when you think about our memories together. But the grief is gone, as you are emotionally now fully realizing that I am alive in my world of what you call heaven and all aspects of what you conceive heaven is like.

You will see me again from time to time at night when your brain waves are pretty much in alpha, instead of beta, like when you are fully awake.

Love,

Suz

Thursday Morning, June 2

For me, with the health condition and infirmities after my operation, although we didn't know it at the time, because neither one of us thought there was life after death, my passing was a good thing. I probably would have had to spend the rest of my life in a wheelchair or at least a combination with a walker, and at sixty-nine, I could not have handled that. At an older age it probably would not have mattered that much, but as you know, I have always been a vital person and loved my work and never would have been that way again.

I would have had to be taken care of, and I may not have ever again been able to swallow properly and might have had to be on a feeding tube the rest of my life. If something happened to you, then where would I be? I think God took care of me, and it was my time to go. I would not have taken my own life because God and my soul had a plan for my life, and it should not be cut short by me prematurely.

A word about suicide: as I mentioned we all have a plan for our lives, and to cut it short is against that life plan. It is my understanding that when a person (soul) comes to our world after taking their own life, there is a period of recovery that, in your time frame, would be like years of soul developing before they would feel the love and joy that the rest of us felt, and that is not a good thing.

However, those that take their own lives are not condemned forever to a lack of love and joy; it just takes some time. Everyone on earth needs to come to heaven in their own time and not prematurely. They must live with God's timing in whatever situation they have. There is a reason for it. It could be a reason for them and their loved ones. I think in your case, in taking care of me, you learned much more about compassion, helpfulness, love, God, and concern, not only for me but for your fellow man.

I am not yet positive about reincarnation. I have not had that teaching yet. If there is reincarnation, do all souls go back to earth to be reborn in able to have learning, or do just some go back, especially in the case of suicide? At some point, all souls stay in heaven forever. This is my surmise, but I don't know yet.

Suz

Friday Morning, June 3

I am on the third level of heaven, as I mentioned, and I have now a small house I can call my own. I can go there whenever I want and just relax and contemplate. I have a garden and, again, it has lovely flowers and plants. I am content. This is accomplished through my mind by thought, but who is to say that everything on earth that seems solid though vibration is not the thought of someone? All this is food for thought, isn't it?

The rest of my time is spent with friends—spirits that I like and want to be with—and learning to develop my general knowledge of this world. I know that it is hard for your ego to accept all of this, but just tell your ego to just cool it.

As I have mentioned, there are no negatives here. I keep harping on love, but God is love, and all the other religions in the East as well as the West tell the same story, although they call God by other names. All agree that something started this world and keeps it going.

Love,

Suz

Saturday Morning, June 4, Another Manifestation

[Last night I was awakened from a dream, and I saw a doorway of a house with a porch and a few steps leading down. This was kind of like on the wall at the end of the bed. I was fully awake. The doorway opened, and out walked a woman who went down the steps. Even though the room was dark, the doorway area was bright and with full color. The woman really was beautiful. I thought she looked like you. She had a complete slender body and had a lovely bright smile. She was wearing a skirt and a sweatshirt. After about four seconds, the scene completely disappeared.]

Yes, it was me. I have now figured out to make my bodily features very attractive so I can show my whole face and body to you. I make myself look like when I was about twenty-four and before you knew me. I was pretty, even though I do say it myself. I know that you were thrilled to see me like that when it has taken several months for me to appear with my full body and face that you really wanted to look at and see. Great, wasn't it?

Suz

Monday Morning, June 6

[I really miss you. This house is so lonely without your presence here.]

I know that you are feeling that way, but as you know, this really was for the best, given the circumstances we both were in.

I really don't have anything new to say now. I am learning all kind of things I didn't know before, such as the making of the universe, how it was started, and why.

There was a Highly Intelligent Force of good and love that was always in the great void of what we call space. It was always there and wanted some company, so it created universes and worlds to enable it to love through humans and other creatures. I know this sounds simplistic, but it is beyond my ability, through you and your being, to create the feelings to describe it further. I think that I have mentioned to you that there are many universes and worlds throughout space. This space we talk about stretches to infinity and beyond. I don't have the expertise of your learned scientists that have been trying to discover all of this so I am very limited in describing to you what I am learning.

[Yes, I just read in the paper that the expanding universe is happening at a rate of 5 to 9 percent faster than scientists had previously thought.]

It is my desire to help you and other people on earth learn how to live a more comfortable, enjoyable life, without the strife you now have. You know my intention while I was with you was to know energy healing to help heal people that were physically, mentally, and emotionally hurting but that wanted and needed to remain living on earth to really enjoy their lives. Well, now I am really developing that skill.

Thursday Morning, June 7

Thank you for buying the plants and flowers for the front yard. You know how I have been into looks so our neighbors will not be upset with our front yard appearance. You can sell my car now if you want, while the summer is here and the weather is good. Just sell it to someone that will take care of it. I am glad that you are going to have the house refinanced so it will make you more comfortable, and if you save money you will have a start on a good retirement. Please plant the flowers. I will leave you now so you can start your day.

Love,

Suz

Wednesday Morning, June 8

[Are you learning any specific subjects?]

Yes, I am learning about the human brain and all that it does. I have certainly a motive since my earthly brain became diseased and stopped functioning properly. Even though your doctors have worked physically with the brain, all kinds of electronic tests and dissection, they still are in the dark about how consciousness, memories, the soul, the spirit, the subconscious, and the conscious work and are interconnected. It is fascinating to me how emotions, joy, love and stress can affect the human mind.

All these secrets are going to help me help others on earth that need and want my help through my being able to relate to them helpful tips for successful living. Of course, this is given through my thought that will just pop up in the mind. Again, I just can't explain in your terms and understanding. Sorry. By the way, through imagination, how that works also.

Thank you for continuing to work on the book. That is coming very well, and I appreciate that.

Sue

Friday Morning, June 10

You mentioned that you have not had a sign from me in the last few days. Actually, I have tried, but your vibrations are low again due to your not feeling really good, with tiredness from that long bronchitis illness and the concern over the two closings coming up. Try and bring your vibrations up by living in the now. Be happy for what you have. Be grateful for what you have, and look toward your future with joy and enthusiasm. You know that I am fine, joyful, and happy, so even though I am not with you physically, you are able to communicate with me like this. I will show you signs in the future just to keep your spirits up, but as you now know, they should not be necessary for you, as you really know that I am alive in heaven with God.

Monday Morning, June 13

[What about another sign like the one I saw of you in the bedroom on the wall, coming out the doorway of a house?]

I can try. That is hard for me to do, as it takes a lot of energy to get my vibration down that low. It is much easier for me to use a bumblebee or a butterfly, but the butterflies are not out yet. You have a lot to do today before you see the doctor about your thumb infection, so it being Monday for you, I am going to let you go. It looks like the book is coming along a lot faster than you anticipated.

Love,

Suz

Make a green smoothie today.

Monday Morning, June 14

[It has been four and one-half months since you passed from this earth. I still think about you pretty much constantly.]

Yes, I can feel it from your thoughts. Maybe I was concerned, when I was ill in the last couple of years of my life, whether you would take care of me if I became disabled. Now that I look back on it, that was my problem. I wondered if I deserved being taken care of since I had that terrible time in college, when my guidance counselor refused, for her own ego's sake, to let me finish the major I wanted and made me change subjects when I was getting top grades. That devastated me, and I, from time to time, remembered that my whole life. My ego took that as a lack of deserving. I now know you would have done anything for me because of your love for me, and you did everything you needed to do and even more so.

Love,

Suz

[I would feel much better if I had another sign from you.]

Yes, and I haven't because you needed your sleep, and I didn't want to awaken you, as the last few nights you have slept six hours straight, and even though you awakened after that you went right back to sleep.

You have needed your rest. When I do give you a sign it is much easier for me to come in the earlier hours of the night, like around 12:00 to 1:30 or thereabouts. This is the time when my vibrations can be lowered enough to come through. It may have something to do with the earth's vibrations at that time of night.

Love you. Enjoy your day.

Suz

Wednesday Morning, June 15

[Hi. How are you?]

I have created mountains and woods by my thoughts, along with some friends I have made.

We are going walking in the woods to see the birds and animals. I am looking forward to it and will really enjoy getting out in the open air from my classes.

I will always be with you, but now is the time to wrap up the book so we can get it out to the ones that need it and others that will read it and start thinking about all of this. My signs to you were dramatic, as I intended to shock you into understanding that there is a heaven, and we all will go there in various capacities after we pass from our earthly lives. Please drink more water. Your body and face will feel and look better.

[Will I ever see or be with you again?]

Yes, you will. I guarantee that. I like you looking at all of my pictures of everything we did. We have a lot of memories even though now it seems short. I know you are feeling better now, and I think your tiredness is just coming up for air after everything that has happened. I will be with you today, but I am going to let you go so that now you can complete your work and start to complete the book.

Chapter 14

FACES, FLOWERS, FRAGRANCES

Thursday Morning, June 16

[What's next? Another event?]

Yes, I will, but I don't know when. The time has to be ripe.

Sue

Monday Morning, June 20

Hi. What do you want to know? I am fine and in good company.

[I really miss you, and I know you are well and happy, but I have great memories of our life together.]

I know that, and I am sorry you are still sad. That will change in time. Just go about your life now and enjoy it.

[Again, what about a sign? Will I ever get another good one?]

Yes, provided you will not dwell on it and continue on with your life. That is my only concern—that you will stay in the past. Show me you won't, and I will continue giving you signs to lift your spirits.

Tuesday Morning, June 21

[I saw your mountain and valley scene twice in a dream last night. Those were your projections by thought where you are?]

Yes, I can make up any landscape I want, and it just as real to me as your earth is to you. Don't you think your earth is made up by thought? It could be thoughts are so deep in man's subconscious through the acts of God's vibrations that it seems so real to you. I don't know myself, as my consciousness, as deep as it is now, still does not have the ability on my level to know the answers to that and many more questions. It is still a mystery to me, and as I progress I will learn all of these things, hopefully.

Again, all of my love.

Sue

I know you really miss me, and you are still upset about the effects of my operation. It was bad, but it is all over now. Talk to spirit guides about anything you want.

[I hope Sue is happy, joyful, and, to a degree, carefree.]

Spirit Guides: [Yes she is, like she has been telling you. She is in heaven, with all that means. She is herself, as you knew her on earth, the same person. She just does not have her physical body that she had on earth; otherwise, all is the same. Who she is, her personality is still there in full form. She loves you deeply and really knows how you took care of her, sometimes to the harm of yourself. If you will do what she says about taking care of yourself, you will be all right and have a long, happy, healthy life yet to go. God will take care of you financially.]

Wednesday Morning, June 22

[I don't understand the loud noise in the bedroom by the buffet last night.]

As you thought, I was trying to get your attention, but you got up instead of waiting to see what would happen. We will try it again at some point in time.

Thursday Morning, June 23

[I know now that you are well and have a new life in heaven, but emotionally it has taken me a long time to feel that.]

I know, but you were brought up to believe, like all people, that death was final. Some people won't, even with all of this evidence of my signs, ever believe the fact that life goes on after death. Don't feel that you have to talk to me all of the time. You know that I am always with you, and as I repeat, I can do everything else that I need to do as well because my thoughts are instantaneous.

Tuesday Morning, June 28

[The other night I awakened to a bright light at the foot of the bed, high up on the right wall of the bedroom. There were seven large, beautifully colored flower heads, each about a foot in diameter, in a line across the wall, just below the ceiling. They were there for only a fraction of a second when I was fully awake. The bright glow had awakened me, and I don't know how long they were there prior to my awakening.]

Hi, yes, I wanted to give you a sign since I had not done that for a couple of nights. You were asking me, and I wanted to oblige you. I am still doing my thing, enjoying my new life and learning to live with my newfound powers. I am still doing the same thing, nothing new. I am resting sometimes in my home, going to class, and resting, talking, and walking with my friends. As you know there is no time here, so there is no hurry. I will be here forever, and as I learn and progress, I will move to a new level in my world, which for all intents and purposes you can call heaven.

Friday Morning, July 1

[Hi.]

Hi, You are finally realizing that I am with you. You have overcome the fact that I am not dead but alive in heaven. Because of your programming all during your life that death is final, it has taken you these five months to get over your shock and grief and know that I am living in another world, and death on earth is not final but a beautiful beginning of life in another world. I am sure it takes many people a lot longer to understand this, and most people that lose a loved one will never realize that they are in a much better place. There I go, using that word *place* again, but it is true.

What a wonderful life I now have. I can do what I want, see who I want, and live the life that I want, as long as it is all tied in with love. You will see some day when you get here. I say again, it is just impossible for me to describe to you what is going on with me now since there are no earthly words or terms that will truly let you feel what is happening to me in this lovely life I now have. Just have faith that I am always with you and will show you that many times in the future. I realize how much you love me and miss me being with you physically, and that is one of the reasons that I love you so much—because you gave me the love that I was looking for all of my life.

It was a shock to me to realize that I was still alive and had transited to another beautiful life. I have lost all of my physical disabilities and problems that I had on earth after my operation, and now I am whole, mentally, emotionally, and physically. I can project my body to be however I want it to be, like my appearance when I was at my best, around thirty-five to forty-five. Enjoy your Fourth of July weekend, and I will start filling you in with more detail about me now as we progress further in our chats.

Love, love,

Suz

[How are you living now?]

I am glad you are asking. Remember we can use our thoughts to make the life we want. I have a small house, kind of like the one we had. I have conjured up, although I don't like that word, my flower pictures. I have an office with a desk where I can write and study. My yard that I can see out of my window is full of flowers of my choice. I can adjust the fragrances that I want. I am not lonely, as I am completely self-contained in my emotional thinking. I can join my friends when we want to get together and swap stories and study. I am living like I did on earth with the exception that I have no physical body to become diseased or hurt. I enjoy love and living, just as I used to, but no emotional downsides. All of my needs are fulfilled by just thinking of what I want. Like I said, there are many universes and worlds that are available to us to go see, provided we are welcomed by similar souls as ours. Some would be so strange that I would not want to go there, even in love, because they don't interest me.

You were asking again about God. On my level of heaven I am learning about God and the higher beings, but all of the mysteries are not open and available yet, as my soul is not developed to that degree. I just know that *all* is here and *all* is love. As I progress in my teaching and training I will know more and will let you know as I know. Don't worry about that for now. You are helping me progress by saying little prayers for me and being over your grief. That makes your vibrations higher and makes it easier for me to contact you. I know that you are still lonely, as I was with you for thirty-three years on a daily basis, doing everything together in a spirit of love and joy. We had a great life together, and I will always remember that.

My memory, if anything, is sharper now than before. I know that you realize that I am with you all of the time—in the car, in church, in restaurants. You just can't see and talk directly with me or hold my hand. I am going to tease you and say *yet*. Who knows? There are many mysteries that I am just learning about since my transition is so new.

[Note: Inserted after the manuscript was completed.] [Several of the books that I have just read state that our deceased love ones can be with us. Suz says she is with me at all times and she can do everything else also. For example, in a book that I have just read by James Van Praagh, an internationally known medium, confirms this to me. It is written "Sandra, your mother is here. She is very close to you and says to be careful of that kitchen knife. "Oh my God" replied Sandra. "I was sharpening it today and almost cut my finger." Was she watching me?" I said "It had to be your mother because I (meaning Van Praagh I wasn't in your kitchen."

Another incident in this same book by Van Praagh coincides with what Suz says, as you will read now in Sue's book that through thought, whatever is wanted in heaven within reason can be materialized. Van Praagh's book states that "She "Grandmother" also says that she loves to look at the beautiful rose pattern on the footstool. Helen wants you to know that she has made a similar one in heaven."]

[Note: James Van Praagh. Talking To Heaven]

I am going to be working here, helping new spirits—souls, people, if you will—with their transition, as I was helped. As you have read in one of your other books, we have hospitals here to receive and rest new people, but most of it is learning unbelievable amounts of knowledge of my world and God's world. I don't know myself what it is all about yet. I don't know why all of this is happening because the knowledge is so complex. The big question I have: why is this cosmos, this universal consciousness, so complex and unique? As I have mentioned before, a first-grader is not able to comprehend higher mathematics. It is a learned and learning experience; that is why it is so fascinating to me.

Love,

Suz

Wednesday Evening, July 6

[Hi. I was reading a magazine about using vitamin CoQ10 to help with protecting my heart, and I was looking up two companies for their pricing. Their prices seemed high, so in my mind I heard the name of another company that advertises they have thousands of vitamin products. When I called them, a recorded voice said, 'Our special today is CoQ10.' Next, a few hours later, I needed to look up someone's phone number that I could not remember and could not find, and lo and behold, the phone rang, and it was that person calling me. Next, I happened to drop my cell phone on the floor, and when I picked it up I found the last twenty-five voice messages were discarded, and the next one left was your voice that I had saved for many months from right after the operation. That one was not discarded.]

Yes, as I mentioned in the first few chapters, I can control things like that for your benefit. Interesting, isn't it?

Thursday Morning, July 7

Hi.

[Hello. That must have been you last night at about 3:30, showing up at the front of the bed in the right-hand corner of the room. You were in all white clothing but in color. Your face was looking radiant and about twenty-five years old. Your hair was cut short but curly, and you had a beautiful smile. I actually heard your voice say, 'Hello, sir.' You were there just about a second, like the flower heads the other night. Then, at about 7:30 this morning, I was awakened by another hello, but I had my sleeping mask on, and when I took it off there was daylight through the skylights, and I didn't see anything of you.]

Yes, that was me both times. I said "sir," as in my mind at that time, I felt twenty-five years old and in my mind was thinking twenty-five. Otherwise, I am my age when I passed on and think like I always have with you—that we are of the same generation, and our fifteen-year age difference did not ever enter my thoughts at any time during our marriage. We were always compatible from an age standpoint. I love you, and that is what matters. It is interesting that the magazines and books you are reading now are all talking about how love is the most important emotion in your world and mine. I am glad that you are learning to relax and are able to sometimes just turn yourself over to God to relax your mind and body.

Love,

Your lovely wife, Sue

Friday Morning, July 8

[I had asked for another sign of some kind, as it makes me feel closer to you, even though I know you are in a wonderful place, and I asked specifically for your fragrance again, as I have not sensed that for quite a while, and it is very personal to me of you.]

[Last night about 12:30 I noticed your and my favorite scent of the sweet lemon shower gel. It was quite strong, as it was a couple of weeks ago, and to me it not only smelled wonderful but it let me know you are there in spirit. Then, about 1:30 I was awakened by a slight tinkle of a glass sound, like a spoon hitting a crystal vase. I immediately awakened, and I saw your face in color, clearly for about a second in the same place at the foot of the bed and high toward the ceiling on the right side. You were smiling, had short curly hair, and looked this time about twenty-eight years old.]

As I had mentioned earlier, you are in pretty good shape as far as getting over your grief, so that makes it easier for me to come to you with some of the signs you like. It is much easier for me to project my face as opposed to not doing that earlier. I know that gives you comfort to have these signs from me so you know that I am still happy and loving my new life.

Suz

Saturday Evening, July 9

[This new book I am reading about after-death communication is a compilation put together by an author of many experiences. It is interesting that what he talks about validates everything you have discussed with me over the last few months, not that I needed that at all. However, it is interesting that these ADC communications are really not very varied and not all over the map. The ones that have them realize, with so many people having the same type of experiences from their loved ones who have passed, that logically shows a pattern of similarity that must be true.]

Yes, that is all true. I am glad that you have reconciled all of my happenings and solidly know that I am alive in spirit form. This knowledge has given you much solace, and I feel that you are not nearly as sad now, just in the last few days. Hooray! This makes it easier for me to come to you with signs and pictures, now that you are feeling much better emotionally. I feel joy for you, and I know that you and I know that tonight, for the first time after my passing, you have felt a little feeling of relief and also a little joy. This is because you really know that I am alive.

Love you terribly much.

Sue

[This new book also mentions a lot of interesting items from after-death communications like you have been describing that the author has compiled, such as that people's spirits that have been there for a while are able to through their thoughts and live in a world similar to earth's but on a much higher vibration level. They have houses, schools, and hospitals, though not like ours. Their hospitals are for people initially resting that are having a difficult time with the realization that they have passed, and there is another life in heaven. It's amazing to me, now that I have gotten in to this, how many instances there are of these communications.

As the author says, many more people have them but are afraid to discuss them, even with their relatives, as they are concerned that they will be believed to be having visions. Many of the spirits want to comfort, but their signs go unnoticed.]

Yes, unfortunately that is true, but maybe this book about my true story will help enlighten any that choose to go further with their interest, like you did, out of necessity.

Chapter 15

MORE CONTACTS AND SIGHTINGS

Tuesday Morning, July 12

[Last night I awakened to a picture in color on the bedroom wall, showing the open dishwasher and a little pan next to it, holding several bars of soap.]

Yes, that was me. I don't like you using the dishwasher soap you bought. It does not get the dishes clean. I wanted you to buy the kind I used to buy, but the only way to show it, as I did not remember the name, was to show you bars of soap so you would know what I want, since you would remember the brand.

[That sounds a little mundane to me since you are not here on earth, and I don't know if you should take the time for such trivial things.]

Actually, I have time, since we don't have any time, for anything that will help you in your life. I want to help guide you to a happy, fulfilled life on earth, so nothing is mundane, using your word. Again, I am here to help you with anything you want, if you ask me, provided it is in my scope to provide it. Only God can provide miracles, so obviously I am limited in what I can do.

Love,

Suz

Thursday Morning, July 14

[I am reading another book about life on your plane, written by a lady that has compiled happenings to tell relatives that are still on earth. They talk about what we have discussed—about your creating what you want by your thoughts if it is through love, and to you they are permanent structures, like houses designed the way you want to live, buildings such as libraries, music halls, schools, and so on. She mentions that the veil between our worlds is very thin, and even though the vibrations are very different, because the veil is so thin, that is why you can come forth for a few seconds to visit me and show me other things. As for me receiving thoughts from your mind, there is no limit to the time since, by thought, you can be many places at once.]

Yes, that is all true. Again, you can't comprehend what is going on with me and what you call heaven due to the low vibrations of your consciousness on earth. Your theoretical physicists are always talking about the vibrational conditions of earth, and what you think is solid is not solid, just wavelengths of energy. Everything is energy; that is why I can come to you and, to a degree, you can come to me. I am never very far away from you, and you would be amazed at how close I am and my world is to you, if you could only perceive it. I think we can get into this topic again when I think how to explain it to you in your terms.

Love you.

Suz

[In reading this new book I have just received, the author talks about your world being very close to earth. Two things, if so, how do our physical happenings affect heaven? It may well be, for example, like a nuclear explosion that goes into the atmosphere. And how close are you?]

Spirit Guides:[Thanks for letting us talk to you again. Please do it more often. Actually, we do not have an atmosphere. Your world and ours is far apart but also close. Let me explain.

Everything is made up of energy. All of the vibrations of love are energy, say, God's energy. Energy can never be lost, but it can be changed. If you could look out your window with our vibrational energy, you would see us. We are closer than you think. It is as if we are in a circle, if you will, although it is not a circle, around your earth. Actually, your earth is within our circle, which is always expanding, as with the universe, cosmos. If you on earth could feel and be with our energy vibrations, we would be on top of each other. That is how close we are to you. Close but far apart, if that makes any sense.

Your wife, Sue, is so close that if you had her vibrations, you could reach out and touch her. That is why some people can feel the touch of their departed ones. They are not dead, in your words; they are alive in a new life, a perfect life. Earth is a trial period for you to help your spirit grow but most importantly help your soul grow to be more like God's image. We could write a book about this, but still you have to take this on faith. If earth were heaven, you could not grow. You need the trials and tribulations of earth to grow. If earth were perfect, how could you overcome any hardships to grow your soul? Earth is the first step in the infinite levels of God's cosmos.

There are many of what you call earths in the infinite universe, but they have different species of life depending upon the planets' makeup. There is a Universal Intelligence of love that we call God, and that is inexplicable to you and sometimes, to a degree, to us. We all take it on faith, however, because we are where we are, and your Suz is where she is. We know and feel the love that is God. Where God came from and who God is—a being of love—that is not completely known, even on our level. As we progress and our consciousness becomes expanded, we will go higher in the hierarchy of God's heavens and will become closer to knowing it.

Angels and higher beings called masters are all-knowing. Because we are where we are, we know there is a God, or we would not be alive here on our plane. We think that because Sue has come to you in many ways from her dimension, that you and we can feel this. You know there is a Higher Source, which, for identification's sake, we call God, as that is the name used in your religions and your Bible. Other religions use other names, of course, for the same entity. This is probably enough for now. Please come again when you want to.]

"Let me ask you another question. What about the book I am reading about how your thoughts can project anything, within reason, that you desire, like houses, buildings, schools, libraries, and so on?"

[As Sue says, yes, we can even project bodies if we want to, but we don't have to. On the other hand, some of us are so used to the appearance of our physical bodies on earth that we are comfortable, even where we are to project ourselves in a body of our choice. As the book you are reading suggests, we like to project a body of how we thought of ourselves at our best period of time on earth. That is about thirty years old. We don't show our age here, as we prefer to look good even here. If a baby or a young person dies on your earth, they come here, of course, and through their spirit, they can also project themselves as any age they want. If they want to still be children, they can. Hope that helps. Good-bye 'til later.]

Friday Morning, July 15

[I had a strong feeling to go to a Mexican restaurant that I have been to before to have an evening meal. I usually go on a weekend, but I felt it necessary to go last night. As I sat down, at the next table, there was a woman reading a book about living on earth and going to the everlasting world of happiness. She saw that I was reading a book on after-death communication, so she said that I should really get this book she was reading. Most people do not read the kind of books that she and I were reading, as the subject of life after death obviously is not a favorite subject. Sue put us together at the same time and place.]

I had you meet her so you could tell her about our church, and she would tell you about the book I want you to read. You had the notion to go to the Mexican restaurant at that time and date. That was no coincidence that she was there when you were there. I brought you two together for the reasons noted above. Enjoy your day. Really, you now know all about love, so please practice it.

I love you and want you to continue working on your real estate business without being discouraged. You are tired. Please walk around the block to help your heart.

Sue

[Can you explain the hierarchy of beings in God's heaven?]

Spirit Guides: [Yes, there are the new arrivals from earth. Then, as they learn and progress in consciousness, they can progress to higher levels in heaven. Next are spirit guides, like us. We are spirits that have lived on earth and have progressed to the point where we can use our earth experience to help and guide individuals on earth, to help them seek their best lives. Next are higher spirits that no longer go to earth to help but can oversee our works.

Next are angels that can go to earth when called upon or when they deem that someone they oversee needs their immediate help. There are higher masters that are next to God and carry out God's wishes. Then we have God, the universal love energy that created everything. In the infinite, ever-expanding universe, there are many other small universes and billions and billions of souls.

It is really beyond your understanding; that is why we do not like to go into this. All will become known someday when you transcend your earthly life. Please don't dwell on this. Just put it into the back of your mind, have faith, and go about your life with love and understanding for your fellow man. Just enjoy Sue's life experiences, and have fun discussing her life as she progresses.]

Friday Evening, July 22

[I just returned from the grocery store, and while in the store an interesting thing happened. In my life I have never had a fly light on me and stay there for a while, although I suppose some people have. This fly was buzzing me and just landed on my hand and stayed there for a long while. It did not try to fly away. This was the only fly that I saw in the store. It reminded me of the bumblebee that sat on my car side mirror on two different occasions. I immediately thought, with a smile, *Guess Sue is showing me she can control this fly.* Since from my readings, spirits can control butterflies, birds, and insects, then why not flies? Actually, one of the reference books talks about a white fly, on several occasions, landing on a person.]

Yes, sometimes I have fun with you and let you know I am around. Again, since everything is energy of some type, we can project a fly as well as a butterfly, or should I say, control a fly, butterfly, bird, or, for that matter, a bumblebee. Since there was not a bird or a butterfly in the store, I used a fly. I knew you would know and feel my thoughts there. Interesting, isn't it? This certainly takes away some of your sadness of not having me physically around. That's why I do this—to let you know I am with you.

Sue

Saturday Morning, July 23

[Hi. Please tell me some of the things you are doing.]

Well, as you know, I have always enjoyed cooking and baking. That is the reason that I have so many cookbooks in the cupboard. During the last few months I bought over the Internet and also had you buy several things for me, like the iron pot and skillet, the small rotisserie oven, and lots of other kitchen items. Unfortunately, I did not get to use many of them.

Now, with my thoughts, I can project and firm up solid my kitchen where I am and have my own cooking show that I have always wanted. I can have my friends that like to cook come visit me, and we can all make things together. We can dream up recipes that you cannot believe that are delicious. We obviously don't eat them like you do. We do not need the food but enjoy the taste, and isn't that what it is all about? I can also interview the great chefs that are here, and we can make things and send the ideas telepathically to cooks that are on earth, and they may sometimes wonder where their inspirations come from. Now you know.

[Right here I want to insert that the books and sources that I have found since Sue's departure all say that thoughts, either by us on earth or thoughts by those on another plane, are able, through vibrations, to make all objects solid. Again, I go back to quantum physics. I am sure that our quantum mechanics studies somehow and in some way will eventually prove this out. In the meantime, this is coming direct from Sue and, like all of the rest of the happenings, prove to me that there are additional inexplicable actions that we can only take on faith. I don't particularly like this analogy, but one of the books says that if we went on a vacation to, say, Bali and came back and tried to explain all of the wonders and sights to the limited consciousness of our pets, perhaps this is where we, as humans, are today. Perhaps this is food for thought.]

I enjoy walks in nature with my friends, seek learning in the halls of knowledge, and attend school to learn the subjects that I love, like biology, energy medicine, and other skills that eventually I can forward by thought to your doctors in the form of their inventions. Where do you think that a lot of the medical breakthroughs on earth come from, as well as other modalities? You have heard that Einstein and other famous inventors have received a lot of their ideas by sitting in silence in meditation and waited for ideas to come through their minds.

[Some of the books I have just read mention that in heaven, in your world, there are beautiful buildings, libraries, homes, schools, gardens, flowers, vast vistas of lands and mountains, everything we have here on earth. One of these books talks about what you touched on earlier—the different levels of the spirit world, heaven, with the astral world being the first level, with the solid—to you by your thoughts—material things such as the buildings, houses, and so forth. This is by the internationally acclaimed author James Van Praagh titled *Adventures of the Soul*, published by Hay House, Inc. Everything I am now reading reinforces what you have been telling me in our conversations.]

Yes, that is all true. We think, and it is. Solid to us as well as solid to you. Everything is vibration, as we have discussed, on our world as well as your world, earth. Ours are just as solid as yours. Most of us do carry our visions of our earthly bodies, as that is what we have been used to all of our lives on earth. It is more familiar to us than to just float around with our spirits, although we can do that as well if we want to. If all of the accounts you read about are similar to what I have been telling you, then you can really believe that it is so.

We also have daily routines that we develop to suit ourselves so that everything can be organized for everyone's benefit. Just like on earth, we want to work for the good of others. Again, if you believe your scientists that nothing is solid, you can start to believe that my world can have all of the earthly goods that you have. As I mentioned, we have a working world like you have, and even though we do not need buildings, food, and nourishment like you have, it is what we are familiar with and used to, so why not? Our physical structures are majestic and beautiful, full of lavish items and vibrant colors—anything we want. Since you cannot see our world, it is difficult to believe in it.

Sue

Tuesday Morning, July 26

[I have again been wondering how we will meet in heaven. Will our love still be there? Then, in the middle of the night last night, I awakened, and the thought came to me loud and clear: *heavenly marriage.* I did not know what that meant, so I went on the computer and found that indeed there was information from Emanuel Swedenborg, an eighteen-century mystic, who wrote that those who have a happy marriage in life will, simply and delightedly, continue the marriage on the other side, if there is spiritual bonding, other than marriage for other reasons.] [Thank you for that thought that gave me the idea to look it up. It answered my question.]

Yes, I know that you miss me very much and have wondered about our relationship when you pass on. Therefore, I sent you that message because I knew you would probably want to know if it meant anything. I am glad you thought to look up the words. That should relieve your mind a little.

Thursday Morning, July 28

[I had not seen any appearance of you for quite a while and was a little concerned about that. Last night I awakened in the middle of the night and immediately saw a brief, small, full-color image of you in full face on the back bedroom wall. You were sitting in what looked like a barber chair in, I suppose, a beauty parlor. You hair was quite thick, and you were probably going to have it cut. You raised your right hand up and said 'Hi, Ward,' which came loud and clear through my mind.]

I know that you were wanting to see me again for assurance that I was still around, so I came through in a way that you would know it was me. I am now glad that you are caught up on your typing so we can now continue our conversations without your feeling strained and pushed.

Love,

Sue

Sunday Evening, July 31

[Over the last couple of weeks I have been having recurring dreams of trying to find a woman that I used to be really attached to. I was mystified that I did not have a face or a name. This was someone that was really familiar to me. I did not have a picture in my mind of a face and did not have a phone number for contact. In my dream, I found myself in an apartment hallway and knocking on a door. No one ever answered the door. I did not know what the dream meant, other that I really wanted to find this lovely person.

I was frustrated that I did not know who I was looking for, but it was someone that meant a lot to me. I always awakened remembering the dream but could not understand it. Then last night, I dreamed that I was on a bus. I was getting ready to sit down on a seat and realized that the woman sitting right next to me finally had a face and a personality. I realized it was Sue that I had been looking for all along. With great excitement we hugged and had a nice, very loving kiss. I had a rush of wonderful emotion that I had finally found the person that I was looking for, and it turned out to be Sue.

When I awakened, I remembered the dream and the wonderful, loving emotion. I still did not know what to make of the dream until I started writing this, at first by longhand. As I was writing, it dawned on me that in my dream, my mind knew that she was missing from my life, and I was looking to find her and continue my life on earth with her. Sue was coming through to show me that I did not have to worry that she was gone forever but that she had moved on and was still with me, although in another way. That must have satisfied my mind, as the dream has not come back.]

Yes, but think of it this way: that is what will happen when you pass on, and we meet again in my world, on my plane. Just feel the emotional relief that you felt when you finally found me in person on the bus in your dream. Take care of yourself, and be loving to everyone you meet and deal with. Show kindness to everyone you meet and love, and make their lives more happy and joyful. After that, we can meet on the same astral plane. That should give you plenty of reason to completely change more than you have, doesn't it?

Sue

Chapter 16

SOME ADDITIONAL THOUGHTS/HAPPENINGS

Monday Morning, August 1

[Why are there so many difficulties on earth, along with the joys and happy times?]

Earth is a learning ground for souls to develop love, compassion, and joy. Many people have to learn these things because they were not born and raised by loving and happy parents and have followed those parents' thoughts and beliefs. God—some call it Infinite Light—is the Creator of the heavens and earth, and everything was created out of love. Because God gave people free will, they can live as they choose, and many live in negative ways.

Heaven, my place now, is all love, happiness, and joy, and that is the feeling of God. Again, God gave earthlings free will; they can do as they want. Think of earth as a training ground—God's training ground. All departed spirits are now love, and since we are love, we wish the best for our loved ones that we have left that are still on earth. We constantly are with you and have advice and help for you, although you have free will and do not have to accept it.

Our communication, as you know, is by thought. A person might have intuition—that is thought actually coming from their departed loved one, even though they are not aware of where it comes from.

[Why are be born on earth and not just in heaven? Maybe it is because we need to develop positive emotional traits and, through a learning experience, change any negative attributes we might have.]

I don't know yet in my own enlightenment. Someday I will know, but it is what it is, and we live with the fact that there is an earth with all the teaching and learning, and there is my place, which is perfect. It is truly a garden of love and perfection, and we live here as we did on earth, without any negative emotions.

Because I love you, I needed to show you that I was not dead but had entered a new existence. This I have done with all of the happenings described in this book and will continue to do as long as you want me to, until you arrive to be with me. This is true for all people. This happens to everyone, although for many people, we are trying to show them that we are not dead but have moved on.

[What have you graduated into doing?]

I am helping little children that come to us after a short lifetime. They come for many reasons, but many times they pass early because they have taught their lessons that they needed to teach on earth. Perhaps their parents, brothers, or sisters needed lessons to help their souls grow while on earth. Babies, both born and unborn, and children grow up here, just as they do on earth. I and my friends help them in crossing over and act like parents here, helping with their growth with love and joy. One of these days their parents will come to meet them, and all will be happy.

One of the reasons I do this is because my childhood was initially one of joy and love, but as I progressed and grew older, I did not feel from the world that I was receiving love. I missed that all-encompassing love and want to give it to my young charges here. Some of my other friends help grownups with their transition and necessary learning issues.

It is hard for you to believe, as I have mentioned many times, but my and our lives here are the same as on earth, but without the negatives that you have and the imperfect bodies. Everything we always wanted or even had on earth is available to us here, in this life on this plane. The old saying that there is more to heaven and earth that we can imagine is so true. That is the reason that you have to have faith.

You must remember that everything that happens on earth is for a reason. The lesson will come out sooner than later as your life progresses. It is a learning experience to enlarge and grow your soul. The soul grows through life's experiences.

A further word about God: although I as yet don't completely know, I am learning God is complete loving conscientiousness that pervades the universe and universes. The latest book that I know you are reading is extremely enlightening about how the new scientists are examining the intertwining of old science, physics, and the study of consciousness. It is explained very well in this book, and it kind of puts together everything I have been discussing with you, my happenings, and your knowledge that you have gained from everything else you have read. It is a very researched book from many different modalities. I am glad you found it. Talk to you later.

Sue

Wednesday Morning, August 3

[Last night I had a dream that Sue was going on a long train trip overnight. We held each other, and she said that it was too bad that we would not see each other for a while.]

Yes, that was me in the dream with you. My long train trip was obviously my dying on earth and renewing my life in heaven. The idea of a long train trip overnight was the knowing that I was going to leave you for a while.

[Sue, thank you for coming to me at night in any way, as it helps me to know that you are around and all right. It makes me getting over your death much easier and helps me with my sadness of you not being here, where we can live together.]

Wednesday Morning, August 10

[Last night I had another dream that I received a phone call from a retired agent who wanted me to talk to people that wanted to sell their house. I drove up, parked the car, and knocked on the door of a modest ranch-style home. I was let in by the woman who had called me. She and a couple were dressed in long white gowns with narrow bright-red sashes around their necks and down the front of the gowns. The woman who introduced me had dark hair and a lovely face and one of the most beautiful smiles I have ever seen. She introduced the couple to me, saying, "These are my friends." They also had beautiful smiles. In fact, all three had really radiant smiles. They were standing in a living room. I said that I would go to my car and get my briefcase. As I left the house, I woke up from my dream.

After I was fully awake in my darkened bedroom, it then dawned on me that the women in my dream who introduced me to the couple who were her friends looked a lot like Sue would have looked at thirty years old and the other two seemed about the similar age. In my dream state, perhaps I was projected either up to Sue's plane, or they were projected down to my frequency level. She was coming through and showing me again that there was truly a fully living life after death. Somehow, she was showing me a glimpse of her world. All three of them seemed totally relaxed and just as friendly as they could be. Again, I believe she was showing me that not only was she alive, but she had friends in what looked like a solid house. To me, the white robes were the giveaway. It seems that maybe these dreams are another way she is communicating with me.]

Saturday Morning, August 13

[Do you think that I will ever see your face again? It has been a while.]

Of course. I will visit you frequently to keep your spirits up. Don't fret about that.

Sunday Morning, August 14

[We have a completely enclosed deck about eight feet high, just outside of the bedroom's sliding glass door and there is a very low level small light outside like a nightlight near the bottom step of the deck. Last night about 12:30, I was awakened by a extremely bright flashing light that flashed about eight times showing through the bedroom shades from a light on the deck. At the same time, there was a loud popping sound. The light flash and the popping sound were together and about probably three seconds apart. It must have somehow come from the low level night light. This is startling to me as there isn't any way that small bulb could have emitted that much light. I knew it was another way of Sue showing me she is still here since all of her signs seem to be different except for her flashing light signs.]

Yes, that was me again. You seem to need me to be around from time to time, and I want to do that. I know that you are now rapidly getting over my loss, even though it may take a year or so for some people to do that. I can feel that you are also getting over your lack of self-confidence and rapidly are becoming your old self.

Thursday Morning, August 18

[Last night I awakened again about 12:30, and after getting up for a glass of water, I went back to bed. After about fifteen minutes, I started to inhale Sue's fragrance, the same scent as before, a lemon-scented body wash that was one of her favorites. At the same time, my body felt a tingling all over that I have felt before when I knew she was around. Some of the books that I have read remark that people have that same feeling. The fragrance became stronger and lasted perhaps five minutes.]

[Thank you for the fragrance last night.]

You are welcome. You had asked me for a few days now about that. You would like me to provide you with that again. Conditions have to be right; by that I mean the vibrations for me to work that fragrance, as opposed to other types of happenings.

[What else is going on now?]

Everything that I had on earth I can, through thought, provide for myself here. I have the same house that I love that I had with you and my same exact Jaguar automobile that I also had. Since I do not have any disabilities, I can drive it anywhere I want.

A word about my abilities: as your scientists have found out, earth and its inhabitants, as well as what seems to be to your permanent structures, are made up of matter, which is made up of atoms. In fact, all earthly doings are just projections, even when they feel solid. Everything is made up of atoms, and the space between atoms is porous. In fact, the human body is matter, and matter is made up of atoms that are far apart from each other. So what you think is solid are atoms with a lot of empty space between them, very porous, so why can't I, in my new world, be able to also project something concrete out of empty space? I do it by my thoughts. Maybe you do it by your subconscious thoughts. Interesting, isn't it?

I believe that everything is thought. Your world and my world is thought, all coming out of God's consciousness. None of this is, at this time, proven by your scientists, although some are expanding their minds to understand the makeup of everything that is solid or that appears solid to determine the nature of energy. Everything is energy, and thought patterns are energy. This is confusing enough to you, so I will stop.

Love,

Suz

[Where will you go from here?]

Actually, nowhere. I am content to do what I am doing, which is living and working in a perfect world. I have previously mentioned about my work. Just realize that as you live, work, and play in your dimension, I am doing the same thing in mine. However, I am also being taught by ancient masters about the workings of the universe, which is developing my consciousness to a higher and higher degree. This will enable me to help all of mankind on earth to understand the mysteries of the universe. Not just me, of course, but billions of souls are working to develop their own abilities in directions they are interested in.

Earth is but a tiny, minute fraction of the total. It seems so solid and permanent to you that it is impossible to see the bigger picture of cosmic life. Someday it will all become known to you, when you come to join me.

Love,

Sue

Friday Morning, August 19

What is it you want to ask me?

[Are you going to start traveling now?]

No, where I will go next I do not know yet. I have no desire at this point to go to any other world in the universe. I am content to live in my house, go to school, and learn to help others wherever they are and with whatever they need.

I know that all of the above sounds like your science fiction, but I can't help that. Everything is true. It is a completely different world that I live in now. It is eternal; there is no death, just a continuing learning about ever-evolving consciousness. You may be tired of hearing that term, but it just describes what is happening in my growth.

I remember your thinking about the first book you read after my departure, about life in heaven. The boy talked about schooling, living in houses, working—all of the things I have talked about. I remember you quit reading it about halfway through because you couldn't believe it from your earthly perspective. Now that I have discussed my life the same way, and the dozen of your books say the same thing, I know that you now, taking everything into consideration, completely believe what happens in my world on my plane.

I can't explain it any better than I have, but I know that you realize now that it is another complete dimension. Again, there is, at this time, not any way that any of what happens on my plane can be proven to you, except that all of the books you read about and from other departed people say the same thing. Even over the years, it should be conclusive to you that the things I have been saying are all true.

Look at it this way: suppose there is another dimension or dimensions other than earth. Isn't it conceivable that all of the examples that we all discuss could be true? It is too bad that in order to see what is going on in the broad scheme of things, people have to have a near-death experience or have moved on through transition from earth. Although if everyone knew for sure that there was life after death in another world, would people on earth have the desire to continue on with their lives, with all of the problems that confront you, in order to learn the lessons that the soul must learn? That is kind of a catch-22 situation.

Good-bye for now, until we talk again later.

Sue

Monday Morning, August 22

[Will I ever see your face again like I have in the bedroom picture you projected in full color or even your whole body like you once did? It has been a while.]

Yes, but the vibrations have to be right. There is a variance in the earth's rotation which makes your and my vibrations sometimes close together, sometimes far apart. Just like the cycles of the moon and stars vary, the earth's vibrations also vary. Just be patient; it will happen, I guess sooner than later. Just as night turns into day, the various cycles of vibration also change.

I am living my life like I want to. I love walking with my friends in the mountains and seeing all of the beautiful flowers and all of the animals. Other than that, I enjoy planting in my garden and watching everything grow, just like on earth. With my thoughts I generate what I want to, as long as it is through love. Everything here is through love. Just like your subconscious thoughts generate your life and your world, mine do too. Again, everything you think is solid is thought-generated. God's thoughts generated the universe to begin with, and though your earth and life appear solid, as you know, the atoms that make up matter are very far apart with a lot of distance between them. It is just beyond your belief that all of the solidness is not solid, but it is so. Again, in your mind this is all science fiction, but it is science and not fiction. What more can I say? Have faith that someday it will all come together for you. Eventually, in many, many years from now, your scientists will prove all this, and your lives will be forever changed for the better.

You were thinking about proving God. God is invisible to you, but the visible proof is all of the seers and prophets that have come down over the centuries. Some of them—Jesus, Buddha, and others—were the visible proof of God's existence. Proof of life after death was Jesus's Resurrection after crucifixion.

As we said in the introduction of this book, we do not want, in any way, to attempt to change anyone's beliefs about God or anything; just hope that some will keep an open mind and, if they want to, do their own investigation, as you have done. If people will think back to what they think are coincidences concerning happenings after their loved ones passed, they may realize that they are not coincidences at all.

As someone yesterday told you, after their mother just passed on, as they were driving, listening to music, the song came on that their mother used to sing to them as little children, "Good Night. Irene." They had not heard that played in years, and since a lot of time has passed, they have not heard it again. When people think back, they may find many such situations arise in their past. Enough for now.

Suz

Chapter 17

ENDING THOUGHTS
ABOUT HEAVEN

Thursday Morning, August 25

[I have been feeling tired, my body feeling a little stiff and having some difficulty sleeping. I went to my doctor and she suggested trying an over the counter product to relax and calm my nerves, just don't take too much and follow the directions. That night I took a pill and still had difficulty sleeping. I arose and took an aspirin. After about three hours of sleep I awakened and thought maybe I should take another aspirin to finish out the night. Previously I had taken an over the counter blood thinner that I have taken nightly for years.

I went into the bathroom to get the aspirin bottle and as I held it in my hand I heard the words in my mind. *Don't take too many aspirin.* I was then hesitant in taking another one but was undecided. All of a sudden the light over the shower enclosure started flashing and then I knew it was Sue watching out for me and did not want me to take another aspirin. I put the bottle down to heed her advice.

After I was in bed a short time I started smelling her favorite fragrance of a lemon body wash which I had not smelled in a very long time. I then felt a little cold for no reason and also felt a little light cool breeze on my face. No window was open as I do not sleep with an open window. There was not any way a cool breeze could normally be felt in the bedroom at night. I then heard in my mind her say she just lightly kissed my left cheek. I had read about sometimes when a departed loved one is with you that the air can feel a little cold and other people have had instances when they felt a light touch on their face. Most of the happenings that I have had other folks have also experienced but this is the first time I have witnessed a light feeling touch. There seems to be a pattern to what a loved one will do to remind you they are around.]

Monday Morning, August 29

[Hi, I still miss you and now only feel sad when I think of all the good times we had together. The sadness is that even though I know that you are alive and well in your dimension I am still here on earth and can't talk directly with you, be with you and touch you.]

Yes, but that is right, however as you dream you will be comforted by seeing me and doing things with me in your dreams. That is one way we can be together since I can project a dream to you in that alpha or deeper dream state and we can join our minds together. Either you are being transported to my vibration level or me to yours or meeting in between. I don't know which yet but we both know that it sometimes happens.

[Do you want to go into further detail about your new life on your plane which we call heaven?]

In my garden outside of my house I can literally plant flowers and things that I want. It is wonderful and my friends can come over every day and we can talk and just be comfortable together. I then every other day go to class where I am studying economics, medicine, math and with this learning developing my consciousness to ever and ever higher levels. As I mentioned I am helping little children who come here realize what has happened and help them find friends and other children to play with. There is not the loneliness that children by themselves on earth feel since all of their systems are filled with joy. No negative emotions here.

My learning is done in the Hall of Learning where all knowledge there ever was has been stored. I have to take it step by step to develop my capacities to realize all there is here. No one can absorb all there is to know very fast, but there is no time and we are here for eternity, there is obviously no hurry. It is just a slow challenging experience.

[Describe your friends.]

We normally are in human shaped bodies as that is what we are used to from our earthly experience. We sit and play games just like you do. However we are all at the age we want to be without any infirmities at all. It is truly heaven as you understand it to be. We still pray a lot and acknowledge God as our loving Father or Mother, whichever you prefer. Nothing is ever boring as there is much to do. Everything you do on earth we can do here and do what we are used to doing in our life on earth. Earth is a training ground for our souls to grow and learn from our earthly experiences.

I don't have the need to show myself as much as you now know emotionally that I am alive and joyful in my new surroundings. That way you can get on enjoying your life knowing that I am always with you. For example, you know now that when you think of me while you are driving that my personality and spirit, me, is sitting in your passenger seat next to you. The same in anything, when you think of me I am there. As I have mentioned before, my being is multi dimensional and I can be with you, and for example studying on my plane. In other words, I can be many places at once. Record your dreams as they will be interesting to others. Goodbye for now.

Suz

[Spirit Guides, what do you have to tell me, if anything, new.]

Spirit Guides:[We are also here with you always, but we want to give Sue preference to you. You love her so much that we don't want to inject our thoughts too much as you know that you can ask her for advice and then use your free will to determine what you want to do. She is content in learning what she needs to know in order to progress to the next higher level which normally takes what you would consider years in your lifetime. She is here forever so there is certainly no rush is there. Just continue what you are doing and wait for what God has for you to unfold.

You will be shown and instructed and led when the book comes out how to proceed from there. You will be called on to do great things in conjunction with the book to help pass the word of life after death to those who not only want it but that need it, living or dying. You can be of great comfort to a lot of people. Just continue reading and studying and become an expert in your field of life after life.]

Friday Morning, September 3

[Last night I dreamed that I was in a large crowded room with people milling around talking with one another and I was looking for Sue. There was a woman that kind of resembled her and as I got closer I realized that this woman was not Sue. In my mind I think that I am still looking for her as she is now gone from me and I want to find her and be with her in person living my life on earth with her again. When I am awake I know that she is alive in heaven, still, in a dream state my mind is not recognizing that fact and I am still looking for her.]

Sunday Morning September 4

[Hi are you there?]
Yes, I am here, always here with you when you want me to be. What do you want to know?
[What is it you want to tell me?]
I am traveling anywhere I want. I can be anywhere in the universes and still be with you as there is no time between distance. I am learning new things about all of God's universes, but I am still continuing my studies and my helping little ones. There are many planets with habitable atmospheres like earths. However there are different life forms depending on the planets makeup. So far none like your inhabitants that I can see. Most are all friendly to us but there are some that don't interest me so I don't go there. There is communication by thought. You call them aliens we don't. They are just spirits like ourselves with their own lives and personalities.

There is one that is light years away but not light years by thought. Thought is instantaneous much like your internet is almost instantaneous. These are apelike inhabitants that are friendly, joyful, just like us but obviously not just like us. When they pass on they have their own heaven. Every living creature in the universe, if you want to use that term, when they pass they have their own blessed eternity.

All this is beyond your scope of belief, but it is true. Just like you vacation to Hawaii, Europe or elsewhere to have and learn about different livelihoods and different cultures we can too. Just think my travels are like my vacation. I hope that helps with some new things.

Love

Sue

[*Note: Interesting that some of our theoretical physicists are exploring the theory that our universe may not be the only one out there. Ours could be one making up a "multiverse", a giant patchwork of universes created infinitely by expanding time-space. While these current concepts stretch our credulity, there is good physics behind this. In fact, some experts have independently pointed to such a conclusion that the existence of hidden universes is more likely than not. This being so, Sue's information is exciting to me to validate this concept.*]

Friday Morning September 9

[Sue, Hi.]

[I just want you to know that I love you very much and I am glad you are where you are, but I am sad that you are not here after thirty three years.]

I know honey, but actually I am with you in your mind when you want me to be.

[I don't know if I will see your face or body again.]

Yes you will but not for awhile. Our vibrations have to be in sync and they will be again someday. In the meantime I will keep being with you in your dreams from time to time. I know you are tired so I will let you go.

Love,

Sue

Tuesday Morning, September 13

[Hi]

I know that you are tired and not feeling well. It has been a long six months now for you since I passed. I know that you know that I am safe, joyful, content and I am in heaven which is somewhat inconceivable to you as you have been taught all of your life that death is final. Your and my churches, then, talk about God and Jesus but they cannot, are not able to communicate the realism to you because unfortunately many of the ministers, priests, etc. just go through the motions themselves. They teach that Jesus died, rose from the dead and is in God's heaven. But if you ask them if there is life after death, most will not believe it themselves when it comes right down to it. Interesting, isn't.

Sue

I am glad your consciousness has really developed and still developing in the form of love for yourself and for your fellow man. Everything is energy and energy is love. God is a loving entity and knows that the universes of his are all based on love. Our souls are pure love but need to expand and grow in unconditional love. As I have mentioned in the scheme of things, which I am not completely familiar with yet, earth is a proving ground for the soul and with free will you have the opportunity to choose the way you want to live and grow. God did not plan to have our souls and thus ourselves perfect. We have to develop our lives to be like his.

Why we were not born as love I do not know yet. Someday I will have that answer and will discuss that with you. As I have mentioned, heaven, my plane and dimension is still a learning world and although we are all in love and joy and with no negative feelings, we still have to develop our consciousness to move up the scale of or should I say levels of heaven. You need to see the positive growth for you even in dire circumstances. There is always a lesson of growth to learn. For everything there is a reason, a purpose. Nice talking with you. You have my undying love always. You took good care of me when I was sick. You were wonderful helping me in the last few months before God took over.

Wednesday Morning, September 14

You were asking me about the interrelationship with me and God and you.

When we are communicating like this or during the day when you think about me, I am always there for you. Now when my vibration wavelength which for me and you is love, your spirit guides and God are also on this wavelength. You can on that wavelength change channels and you can talk to your spirit guides and also commune with God. As you know God's essence is everywhere with everybody. Tuning in is the problem for most people and that's why prayer is so effective. With prayer it is a definite time that people can take the time to not only express their desires to help anyone they want to, but also to help themselves. God listens to all prayers in a way that is best for them. Thanks for talking with me today. I will let you go about your business.

Love,

Sue

Tuesday Morning September 20

I love you still. I will always love you. You took care of me when I really needed it. I always wondered if you would but I should have known from your love that you would. I just wanted to reassure you that I am here for you. You have been concerned that I was going on, but when the vibrations are right you will see me again. In the meantime I am coming to you through dreams and we are together again that way. That should give you some satisfaction. Please let God take care of you. You are worrying too much about the future. That is all I wanted to say.

Love, your wife for eternity.

Suz

Friday Evening, September 23

Spirit Guides, again.

Spirit Guides:[You are worrying too much about the future and not letting God handle it for you. Just step out of the way and quit trying to do things all by yourself. You, all of your life have many times paddled upstream when you should have floated downstream. Things always turn out for the best, but sometimes it is hard to see that when things go wrong. Just relax and let the world go by. That is not to say quit trying. Sometimes you try and try and then when the timing is right everything seems to fall into place that is what is happening now. You have gone through the most trying time in your life, losing your best friend, companion and true love. You know that she is all right in her new life, but emotionally it is sometimes hard to believe that.

Just keep on doing what you are doing work wise and everything shortly will change for you. We know it has been a tough year but the year will go by and there will be a new year for you that will put everything that you have gone through into perspective. Everything happened for both you and Sue for the better. She was not really getting much better and did not look forward to the future, because of her nerve problem she might never learn to swallow again. Someone would have to take care of her and since her lifespan even with the operation would be longer than yours, when you will have gone what would she have had to do to even live a potential normal life.

She probably could not have enough to live on and potentially could have been a ward of the State. That would have been a miserable existence for who knows how long. By God loving her and by evidently her learning in her lifetime the lessons she was supposed to learn, God took her into his fold forever. Someday you will join her and you will both be together again. You must have some life lesson still to learn or possibly God wants you to do something that has yet to be presented to you. Possibly this book when published will be a turning point in your life and just may teach you to help other people that are or will be in your situation in regards to their loved ones. God works in what to us seems mysterious ways.]

Good luck,

Your friends.

Monday Morning, September 26

[You know I have not seen a picture of you at night or smelled your fragrance for a while. I hope that I am not being selfish.]

No, you are not being selfish. You are still emotionally hurting after your loss of me on earth. It has only been a few months and this is natural. You know that I am joyful and having the time of my life now. I don't mean to be flippant, but I want you to realize that I am happy and here for you whenever you want. If you would just relax and just realize that I am just on the other side of the curtain from you and we can communicate you could relax and other than just intelligently know I am here, you would emotionally know it also and your life would turn joyful again.

Take your life in stride now and you will be able to once again to do what you want and what has to be done with ease. My whole other world is waiting for you when your earthly life is over, but only in God's time. Like all of the books and guru's say, if you would just take a few minutes every day to pray and meditate early in the morning and before you start your day, your life would smooth out and you would be happy again.

I should come to you at night and in some way hold your hand and you would know it was me. I really don't know if I could get my vibration down that low to meet yours. I have been here in my world long enough that my vibrations are higher than when I first came and it is more difficult for me to come through to you in any visual way like I have done. That is why some of your books say that as time goes on visitations are less frequent. That is new in that your information does not tell you why, but the increase in vibrations for me is why. Hope that makes sense. Our communicating like this is not affected because it takes very little effort on my part to come through your mind.

On another note, your brain is like a computer, it does what it has to do to keep you alive and flourishing. On the other hand, your mind which is your personality, your spirit and your soul is your consciousness that continues on after your physical death. This is why I am still me, the me that you knew and still now know. As I have mentioned many times now, please take the time to do your love prayers several times a day and your physical health will improve. God will heal you as your body is programmed to heal itself. If you will let God help you get rid of your stress through meditation, prayer, if you will, there will be a cure. Let you go now.

Always yours,

Sue

Tuesday Morning, September 27

[What is going on now?]

Tom and Jerry are here with my dad and uncle. These are not the ice cream folks (pun), they are a couple of my old friends that I knew on earth who just happen to be Tom and Jerry. There are other relatives and friends that I see from time to time. I am making new friends all of the time. There of course is no hostility or negatives. We all enjoy each other's company just talking and discussing the knowledge we are getting from other schools. Everyone seems interested in other endeavors. There are streets and buildings sort of like old cities and buildings in your Europe since we are a mix of nationalities.

There is playtime, I love walking and the mountains. I am learning about the complete extent of the universes and all of the exciting inhabitants of all of the different planets that God has created. Everything is bright and beautiful and of course we do not have any weather here, but all of the planets that have life have some kind of climate just like earth has. Everything is so immense that on this level of heaven I don't have the complete picture of the whole complete scheme of things. There are many mysteries that I have to learn. It may seem strange to you but we still don't know the whole complete reason and if you will, thinking of God's plan.

We are in a dimension of love and joy, just unbounded love that permeates everything and all of us. I do know that this is what it is all about from my perspective. Nothing boring, every moment is a new delight. The main purpose is learning to be able to help the inhabitants of earth grow in their consciousness and also health and well being, love and joy. As I have mentioned our plane is based on our life as humans on earth. Every intelligent life form in the universe has their own "earth" and when they lose their physical being they have their own heaven. Like I said, I am not aware of the whole scheme of things.

Sue

Friday Evening, September 30

I know that you are just getting back to normal after my demise from earth. It was a great shock to you to have me die and even a greater shock to me when I did and even a greater surprise that I was not dead but still alive arriving in heaven. You know that I am happy and everything here is love. We are all living in love. God's love, as I have mentioned there are no negatives. It is a wonderful situation that I am now in so although you miss me and will the rest of your life we will be together again. Please remember that and your life will again be happy and joyful.

Just enjoy your life now and I know you have really changed in your consciousness to want to help other people in their sorrow. When the book comes out you will have something to work with without just trying to tell people verbally about your situation with me and what has transpired. In print it will be a complete story of what has happened to both of us.

You know now for sure that there is a God, a loving Entity that has created the heavens and the Earth. You also know that it is not only possible but that happened. Why, because I am proof that there is an afterlife with communication skills and be able to communicate with you in loving ways. Again, I am me, my personality, spirit and soul.

Tuesday Morning, October 4

[Why does the soul need growth to grow?]

God and the soul are intertwined. The soul is the deeper part of you, your essence. We all have a life force in your earthly life as well as in the afterlife. The soul is a part of this life force just as your personality, your mind and your consciousness is a part of your life force and is the connection to God. When you pray you actually pray to God through your soul although you don't know it. The essence of who you are as an individual is contained in your soul. Look up the definition of soul in your computer and write it down here to help express what I am saying.

[*Note: Soul, the principle of life, feeling, thought and action in humans. Regarded as a distinct entity separate from the body and commonly held to be separate in existence from the Body, the spiritual part of humans as distinct from the physical part, the spirit and essence of a person. An example of your soul is the part of you that will go to Heaven and be immortal according to the teachings of certain religions.*]

When God created you, you were a spark off of his flame and you developed into a personality like a baby grows into an adult, but the growth of you continues forever unlike the growth of you on earth. There are wondrous things in God's universe and earth is just a starting point for growth. There are areas of life to come to all of you beyond your imagination. I am only now seeing just part of the big picture of life. You think your life on earth is all there is, but it is just the beginning of a great joyful, loving adventure.

As I have said before it is just unexplainable to you now. Just have faith in your total future. You didn't think that we had anything to talk about, didn't you.

I am glad we met although it was really meant to be and our life on earth together is and was the beginning of a long love affair that someday will open up for you. Just keep your goodness and use the Golden Rule every day.

Love, your wife

Sue

Wednesday Morning, October 5

[Tuesday night I had another dream about Suz leaving on a trip kind of like the dream earlier when was going on a long train trip. This time it was an airplane. She and I were going to an airport where she was catching an airplane however the airport was older and the airplanes were older. The airplanes were still loading on the airstrip through a tall rolling ladder like they did many years ago with a Douglas DC-3 and the typical row of windows. Her flight was three o'clock in the afternoon and we were running a little late. After she boarded and was seated I was able to look through the window and saw her seated. Her physical appearance was about a young fifty years old. She was well dressed and with her usual bright smile.

After the airplane started rolling down the runway, I followed it in my car for a long, long way before it took off. I knew that I would never see her again so I followed as long as I could. The plane was a little late and took off just after three o'clock. I then awakened and it dawned on me that she passed away in the hospital just after three in the afternoon. This was all a dream but somehow it must have tied into my memory of the time.]

Sunday Morning, October 9

[Last night I awakened about twelve midnight and lying in bed in the dark I was going over the day's events. All of a sudden with my being fully awake, I heard a loud ding dong doorbell sound at the foot of the bed. Our doorbell rings in the hall and has a much softer, lighter tone. Never the less, I went and looked out the door and no one was there. Then I went into the master bathroom and turned on the light. After a minute the lights, one in the shower enclosure and two in the ceiling of the bathroom went out momentarily and when they came back on the one over the shower started flashing on and off, bright and then dim. I knew that for sure it was Sue telling me that she was with me.

For several days even though we communicated by mind conversation, I had not had an occurrence like those I had before. I had been thinking that I really wanted that type of assurance that she was still around in my world and so it finally happened again.]

Yes, that was me. I had waited until my vibrations were low enough to where I could give you another demonstration. It is easier for me to use the lights and a noise like in this instance a doorbell than to show myself or even produce a fragrance. It takes a much different stronger vibration to achieve more than lights and sound. I can tell you feel much better after a demonstration from me.

As I have mentioned, I am always around for you and go wherever you go. If you ever move to another location in the city or even the country I will be with you whenever you think of me and also do everything that I have and want to do.

Love,

Sue

I think now is the time to wrap up the book, as we could seemingly go on forever, as long as we remain in contact, which we will, but I really would like my story to get out there as soon as possible to hopefully help others with their devastation and grief after their loss. So long for now.

Love,

Suz

A Final Word about Contacts

[After Sue's contacts to me started happening, and thus my need to find out what was happening, I located the reading materials that I could find on after-death communication. It is now my belief that all after-death communications are through love vibrations. It does not have to be unconditional love, but there has to be some love between the departed, as well as those left on earth, in order to have the vibrational wave lengths necessary for the communication in any of its forms. If there is no love, there is no reason for the communication, as neither party has invested any emotional feeling. If there is no grief or sorrow in the form of love, then why would a departed soul—or, for that matter, the ones left behind—have any interest in a contact at all?

Most contacts are designed to remove or mitigate the sorrow and grief of the ones left behind. If there is love, the departed will always try to come through some channel, but if the person to receive does not believe or is not aware of the attempt at communication, then nothing will happen.

Again, please be aware that the spirit and personality always tries to come through in some manner. Whether through electrical manifestation, voice, dreams, sounds, or visualization, they will always try to come through. Many times the receiver will not be receptive to the vibrations because of disbelief, fear, or concern over something that they believe is not happening or just lack of understanding the need for mutual vibrations. Many times afterlife communication may come through unusual channels, such as an item left in an unusual place, a bird that comes extremely close, or, as in my case, several instances of a bumblebee where a bumblebee should not be, and the recipient will just dismiss them as a coincidence.

The departed vibrations are much higher than the dense vibrations of earth, and that is why many manifestations can happen at night, when earthly vibrations may be raised due to a slow-down in the activity of the mind. The vibrations have to be adjusted down from the departed and adjusted up from the denser vibrations of earthly minds, again automatically from the inactivity of the earthly mind at rest.

One of the many ways receiving may happen is through meditation. Some of the books listed in the recommended reading list that I have compiled at the back of this book show ways of meditating. If all else fails, another way is through a medium that is well known and respected.

So please, if you are not receiving from a loved one, do not be discouraged. Realize that the loved one always wants and tries to come through. There are many instances of communication happening long after the death of a loved one.]

In Conclusion

---◆◆◆◆◆◆◆---

First, I wish to thank Ward, for in his terrible situation of my passing unexpectedly, he recognized in that first week that something out of the ordinary was happening. Instead of ignoring and writing it off or fearing it, he started really investigating it with his usual thoroughness and persistence. Also, I want to thank him for his taking the time practically every day to journal with me, write it out by longhand, and then spend many hours, night after night for over four months, typing this up in book form.

It was my intention from the beginning to tell my story to anyone who will listen to help them over their shock and devastation of losing a loved one. Even in the instance of someone's relative, spouse, son, daughter, or friend that has been ill for some time, and they know that the inevitable will happen, it is still a shock to lose them when that time comes. God also wants this story told to help alleviate the suffering that happens when a loved one leaves this physical earth that has been a necessary growth time for our souls.

I was driven to develop all of the signs noted in this book, not only to help Ward's situation but to show anyone else that will take the time to follow up and believe that life still goes on. All departed wish to give signs to their loved ones, but many times the signs are not recognized for what they are. People can sometimes dismiss them as coincidences. It also depends on how much grief the departed feels from the ones left behind. Sometimes there is no need for any intervention in their lives, as their lives go on without much of a problem.

I myself was dumbfounded when, after my difficult time in the hospital, on the day of my passing I found myself not dead but transported to a completely different life in heaven. As I have mentioned many times, heaven is beautiful, and I can and have been involved in reinventing my new life here.

Please enjoy this book, and if you need this help, so be it. Otherwise, I know that anyone who picks up this book will at least, hopefully, benefit from what is written here and will rethink their beliefs and further investigate this by perhaps reading some of the books in the reading list.

Thank you for your attention. Love to all of you.

Suzette Delashmet Shockley

[For me, I feel that I have completely changed my attitude about God and the afterlife. Up to now, I had hoped that there was a Supreme Being that created all of this that we are aware of, but now, after these several months, I know that it is so from Sue's activities and communication with me. I now realize that there is life after death, and that on earth we are loving mortal beings. This has given me a rebirth in my thinking and behavior toward myself and toward my fellow humans.

I now feel that love is the most important emotion, and I am trying to see and feel love in everyone I meet in my everyday activities. At least try to see that everyone has a spirit that needs to expand through love, and what little I can help, I want to do so. I am no longer just thinking mostly about myself and my needs. Being human, sometimes this is a challenge, but I try to bring myself back to this knowledge and dedication. At least with Sue, I was more concerned about her needs, especially in these last couple of years, than my own. I know that death, as we know it, is not inevitable and that our physical bodies will die but who we are lives on.

Thank you for reading this material that has come through my almost daily journaling, as well as reading about the manifestations. It is also interesting that a few of my notes came to me at different and odd times, when I know that she wanted to come through to me with her thinking at the moment. Some of these notes were made on napkins while eating in a restaurant and others while I was driving, and I had to pull over to write them down.

The subject of death, in many instances, is a subject that most people will not or do not want to think about. Many of the readers of this book may not acknowledge what is said here. That is all right. The intent of this book is not to try to change anyone's mind about their beliefs of death. The whole purpose is to try to give insight to the possibility of at least thinking about the subject of life after death. As such, this may help alleviate the grief of loved ones left behind. In some instances, it may help those that are in their last stages of life to realize that death is not final.

Sue's and my contact will continue, but at some point, as she says, we need to stop and develop this record in print. I hope this has been done.]

Ward Edward Barcafer Jr.

SUGGESTED READING LIST

Anderson, George and Barone, Andrew Walking in the Garden of Souls. GP Putnam Sons. A Member of Penguin Putnam Incorporated, New York, New York. 2001 George Anderson's advice from the Hereafter for Living in the Here and Now

Calvi-Parisetti, Preio MD 21 Days Into The Afterlife. OpenMind Publishing -December 2008. A scientific and literary journey that may change your life.

Crandall, Dr. Chauncey M.D. Touching Heaven. Hachette Brook Group 2015 New York, New York. A Cardiologist's Encounters with Death and Living Proof of an Afterlife.

Frederick, Sue Bridges to Heaven. St Martin's Press 2013 New York, New York. True Stories of Loved Ones on the Other Side

Greaves, Helen Testimony of Light. Penguin Group New York, New York. 1969 An Extraordinary Message Of Life After Death

Guggenheim, Bill and Judy Hello From Heaven. Bantam paperback edition April 1997 New York, New York. Have You Ever Been Contacted By A Loved One Who Has Died? A new field of research-After Death Communication-confirms that life and love are eternal.

Neal, Mary C. To Heaven And Back. Waterbrook Press 2011 Colorado Springs, Colorado. A Doctor's Extraordinary Acount of Her Death, Heaven, Angels and Life Again.

Northrop, Suzane Everything Happens For A Reason. NorthStar 2 LLC 2004 New York, New York. Love, Free Will and the Lessons of the Soul.

Rohde, April The Gifts They Leave Behind. 2013 April L. Rohde.

Van Praagh, James Talking To Heaven. Penguin Group 1997 New York, New York. A Medium's Message Of Life after death.

Woods, Walda Conversations With Tom. White Rose Publishing 2000 2001 North Andover, Maine. An Adventure in After-Death Communication.

The Narrow Gate Painting. Lovely painting shows when it is time, drop our baggage and ascend.

http://sonya-shannon.com

CPSIA information can be obtained
at www.ICGtesting.com
Printed in the USA
FFOW04n1111200117
31541FF